LEANING ON THE INVISIBLE

For Carole (with an 'e')
All very best wishes
and love,

Love + Light,

Margt.

Mary Bowmaker

'Mary Bowmaker's thought-provoking book *Leaning on the Invisible* provides true life stories skilfully woven into a narrative that gently guides the reader towards the realisation that we are much more than just flesh and bones created by some happy cosmic accident but we are in fact, at the very core of our essence, spiritual beings expressing ourselves through a physical body. All serious spiritual seekers should add this book to the top of their reading list.'

Dr C Bowman

Leaning on the Invisible

by

Mary Bowmaker

COURTENBEDE

Copyright © Mary Bowmaker 2012
First published in 2012 by Courtenbede
c/o Loundshay Manor Cottage, Preston Bowyer
Milverton, Somerset TA4 1QF
Answerphone / fax: 01823 401527
e-mail: amolibros@aol.com
website: www.amolibros.co.uk

Distributed by Gardners Books, 1 Whittle Drive, Eastbourne,
East Sussex, BN23 6QH
Tel: +44(0)1323 521555 │ Fax: +44(0)1323 521666

British Library Cataloguing in Publication Data
A catalogue record for this book is available from the British Library.

ISBN 978-0-9554292-1-7

Typeset by Amolibros, Milverton, Somerset
This book production has been managed by Amolibros
Printed and bound by T J International Ltd, Padstow, Cornwall, UK

About the Author

A FORMER PROFESSIONAL musician, both teacher and performer, Mary Bowmaker has always loved writing, small successes over the years encouraging and inspiring her to write her first book *A Little School on the Downs*; a record of the life and work of a headmistress and her school in Victorian England, and her successful *Is Anybody There*, her first book about the paranormal.

Contents

List of Illustrations

This book is dedicated to my wonderful, darling parents

Mary and Stephen Wilton

and to

My Beloved Husband Peter R. Bowmaker

and Toby

Acknowledgements

My thanks to:

The Religious Experience Research Centre, otherwise known as the RERC, University of Wales, Lampeter, Ceredigion. My thanks for the opportunity to delve into fascinating and in-depth accounts of true experiences, and, in particular, I would like to express my appreciation of Anne Watkins, always helpful and ready to assist with research, her thorough knowledge of the archive being invaluable.

Jane Tatam from Amolibros, for being so understanding and appreciative of the subject. Once again Jane, thank you for 'being there'.

BBC, Radio Four. The wide range of programmes, and always seeming to be broadcast at just the right time for me, has been remarkable in both supplying me with new material and reinforcing much of what I already had.

Diane and Keith Robson for their friendship, and for acting as my 'Technical Advisors'.

Sylvia Povey Kennedy, friend and for her 'diligence and time' acting as 'reader' for me.

Iris Wilding, Medium and Healer and good friend who has given me hours of her valuable time chatting, discussing, and pondering on the deep and even deeper questions of 'life', and 'death'; and who, carefully and sincerely, often advised me on the correct usage and terminology with regard to 'Healing' and 'Spirit'. Thank you, Iris.

Linda ——, who came along, 'out of the blue', with such amazing and beautiful photographs, giving them to me for *Leaning on the Invisible* from her heart, and for being a 'new found friend' in so many ways.

To those readers who have taken time to add their own thoughts and experiences, at the back of their copy of the book, I wish I could read them all!

And last, but by no means least, to my friends and acquaintances and strangers (remembering that a stranger's just a friend we don't know) who have so willingly and trustingly given me their own experiences, and which they have allowed me to publish, thank you.

Sincerely,

Mary Bowmaker

Foreword

For over four decades I have researched what people often refer to as 'the paranormal', 'the preternatural' or 'the supernatural'. For the last six years I have done so on a professional basis, and now make a living investigating and writing about events and experiences that simply do not fit in with a materialistic view of the world we live in. I now need no convincing that there is far, far more to our universe than most people imagine. There was a time when I was consumed with desire; the desire to convince people that the physical world is married to an invisible, far less substantial one that most people are oblivious to. I no longer do this, and it may be appropriate for me at this juncture to explain why.

There are two kinds of people in this world; there are those who possess what we may call a 'spiritual nature', and those who don't, or at least, don't seem to. The truth is that we all possess a spiritual nature; it is just that in some people it has yet to be awakened. I have learned that it is impossible to energise or awaken the spiritual aspect of others simply by employing the technique of intellectual conversion. Samuel Butler, in his poem Hudibras, said,

> *He that complies against his will*
> *Is of his own opinion still*
> *Which he may adhere to, yet disown,*
> *For reasons to himself best known.*

And it's true. Logic, facts and evidence are simply not enough to unseat a deeply held belief (or lack of it) or a powerful conviction based on instinct. We may bully people into accepting our own convictions, and they may then outwardly espouse a conversion to them, but, deep down inside, they haven't changed at all. What we have engineered is not conversion, but its dark twin, *compliance*. True conviction is carried not on the wings of intellectual conversion, but on the wings of a deep, spiritual conviction. The New Testament contains a remarkable example of the difference between the two:

> *When Jesus came into the coasts of Caesarea Philippi, he asked his disciples, saying, Whom do men say that I the Son of man am? And they said, Some say that thou art John the Baptist: some, Elias; and others, Jeremias, or one of the prophets. He saith unto them, But whom say ye that I am. And Simon Peter answered and said, Thou art the Christ, the Son of the living God. And Jesus answered and said unto him, Blessed art thou, Simon Barjona: for flesh and blood hath not revealed it unto thee, but my Father which is in heaven.*
>
> Matthew 16; 13-1

Simon Peter had not undergone an intellectual conversion and come to the conclusion that Jesus was the Son of God on the basis of the facts – a 'flesh and blood' conversion – but, *as* Jesus himself pointed out, due to a powerful revelation gifted to him by God. It is this type of spiritual conversion that buries itself deep inside our soul, and simply cannot be shifted. One does not have to be a Christian or Bible-believer to embrace this concept; it is a universally recognised phenomenon within all religious traditions.

The truth is that attempting to convince people of something before they are ready is an exercise in futility. Until they have had their own, personal 'revelation' they will never be truly converted, no matter what they say in public.

Sometimes, however, that spiritual revelation may find its way to us via an ostensibly 'flesh and blood' route. We may hear something uttered on the TV or radio which suddenly precipitates within us a profound change in our thinking. A heart which has been hardened for decades may instantaneously be softened by its owner simply glancing upon a tear in the eye of another. Observing an act of true heroism may convert someone who is consumed by cynicism into an optimist who comes to embrace the belief that there truly is goodness in other people if we but take the time to look for it. Or, we may read a book.

In my experience, it is not always events of great political or historical importance that change people, although they certainly can do. Often, it is minor, almost trivial events which, to coin a phrase, hit us like a ton of proverbial bricks and make us completely rethink our perception of the world around us. To give an example, I once met a man who went through a profound religious conversion to Spiritualism because he'd had a dream in which a deceased uncle appeared to him and smiled. The uncle hadn't said a word; he'd just smiled – but there was something about that smile which invaded the man's soul and changed him from within. Another chap I know was on the brink of committing suicide. Just then, he heard music drifting from the window of a nearby house; it was the band Westlife, singing 'I Have a Dream'. Something about the words took hold of him. He cried, and then realised that his life was actually worth living. All he had to do was make changes.

Leaning on the Invisible is a powerful book; the sort of book that can act as a conduit for that intangible but powerful spiritual essence which can take hold of us, reshape our mind and energise our soul. *Leaning on the Invisible* is also a unique book, for despite the powerful evidence within it pointing to the existence of a 'world of spirit', the author, Mary Bowmaker, never once resorts to the classic tactics employed by many authors to infuse the reader with her own ideas. Neither does she heavily employ classic arguments so beloved of theologians and Divines. Yes, she nails her metaphorical colours to the mast, sets out her spiritual stall and waves her theological flag; but Mary Bowmaker does this in a gentle way, a way that allows the reader to read without feeling threatened, imagine without feeling bullied. *Leaning on the Invisible* is a treasure chest of enigmas; each page – indeed, every page – presents us with stories. There are strange stories of people who have had odd or quirky experiences which, seemingly, have no rational explanation. There are others stories of people who have had 'mountain-top' experiences that are anything but trivial. Mary Bowmaker presents them all without resort to long, detailed sermons or the introduction of unnecessary detail. The reader is simply presented with the facts and a short commentary – and then left to wonder.

Charles Fort (1874 – 1932) was an American researcher who had a fascination with bizarre phenomena. In his books he listed hundreds of odd occurrences, and the term 'Fortean' is now used routinely to describe all any supernatural or paranormal events. Mary Bowmaker follows in the tradition set down by Fort, but with one important difference; she infuses her narrative with an aura of spirituality that will give the receptive reader an option; the opportunity to advance into the vista of unexplained phenomena and grasp hold of a crucial truth; *this life is not all there is.* Beyond this 'Vale of Tears' there is another plane of existence which, at some time, we will all be required to visit. *Leaning on the Invisible* is a fascinating introduction to the unknown, a portal into another world which, if we fail to walk through it, leaves us immeasurably impoverished.

I have met Mary Bowmaker personally. She speaks with

sincerity and insight. She possesses a largeness of heart that makes her the perfect person to pen this wonderful tome. She has made an important contribution to the growing library of literature in this genre, and should be commended. Although Mary does not use this book as a vehicle for pushing her own beliefs on anyone, I will be surprised if even the most dyed-in-the-wool cynic can reach the last page without being moved to question their disbelief in the unseen. *Leaning on the Invisible*, you see, offers a gift of immeasurable importance; hope. Superbly written, I commend it to the reader as one of the finest books of its kind, and even that compliment does not really do it justice.

Michael J. Hallowell West Boldon,
April 21, 2011

About Mike Hallowell:

He is the author of many books, his first one being *Herbal Healing*, released in 1985.

He writes regularly for a number of journals and newspapers including writing the longest running weekly paranormal column in the *Shields Gazette*. Mike has starred in a number of documentaries about the paranormal, including *The Ghost Detective*, *Uninvited Guests*, and *Anatomy of a Haunting*. He runs his own media business and regularly appears on BBC radio and other channels here and abroad. Mike has Native American heritages and teaches and lectures on *The Medicine Way* throughout the UK.

Prologue

Leaning on the Invisible tells a story, a true story, but perhaps unlike most other true stories you may have come across, you and I are the players; we are the players, the main characters, as together we chart what should be the most exciting, fascinating and rewarding adventure we will ever embark on...our quest to find Spirituality!

Spirituality, such a difficult word to understand, a difficult subject to come to terms with – but *is* it?

Leaning on the Invisible is a story full of questions where we ourselves discover the answers; a story that turns life into a thrilling paper-chase as we follow one lead after another, one truth after another, amused and often 'amazed' at outcomes; enriching life with purpose, with meaning and with the conviction that we do not travel this road alone.

It is a story of the unbelievable made real.

One of the questions we might like to consider is, why do non-believers, often pure agnostics, 'scoffers', ridiculing the very notion of 'something' out there, ('God', the 'Universal Energy', the 'Life Force', 'Creator'), fall on their knees begging for help in times of 'desperation' – but they do! Plead with an 'invisible' force to save them.

And how is it that martyrs, martyrs from every age, suffering the most brutal, horrific tortures, bravely bare up, unflinching in their belief of something they cannot see but know, with every fibre of their being, is 'there'.

Talking with people today, and certainly not particularly church-goers, or those who are 'religiously minded', but talking with people, in just a casual way, as you maybe meet on the street, on a bus or in the shops, it is remarkable to find that so many of them have a true understanding and interest in the 'so-called' paranormal. Many have a story to tell, an experience they are not afraid to relate, a great belief in 'angels', and a belief that 'yes', there *is* 'something', and a reason for everything.

The world is changing fast and we know it. No one can escape the consequences or deny that our whole way of life, the very fabric of life, is changing. Changes have been in evidence since the sixties, both subtle and dramatic, and all heralding in the new age, The Age of Aquarius, also known as The Age of Enlightenment. Prophesied to be the age of the 'spiritual revolution', where we turn from being a greedy 'me' society, (therefore raising our consciousness to the 'higher' side of life), to one of caring and sharing. To an age of 'global understanding', belief in the 'Brotherhood of Man', and recognising the fact that we all, indeed *all* life, comes from the same spiritual source.

It was also prophesised that in this new age of Aquarius, an Avatar, a Saviour, a teacher, would return to earth to be a 'light' in the world during these dark times, showing us a 'better way'. However, as we slowly but surely turn our thoughts, raising them to the highest and best of what it means to be truly human, could it be, according to another prophecy, that the Avatar, the Saviour, the teacher, the 'light', is coming from 'within'?

Through modern technology, and the social networking skills happening along with it, we are experiencing what are probably the greatest changes ever, to life on our planet.

President Nelson Mandela of South Africa recognised the value of the new technology back in 1994. At the end of a speech to the U S Congress, he said:

'New technology will do what all the great thinkers failed to do – prove that we are all part of one, indivisible and common humanity.'

Social networking; communicating with each other, the friend along the street, the relative we rarely see, the stranger at the far side of the world: ordinary people communicating in a way that hasn't happened before, and in so doing, setting up a system of 'information passing', a means of 'pass it on' power, affecting every area of our lives. Happening now, in this the Age of Aquarius, bringing us closer, ever closer, to the Brotherhood of Man, to the 'spiritual side of life', the 'inner teacher'...if the prophecy is to be 'fulfilled'.

Now we are ready to move onto the first line of the first chapter of this book.

Chapter One

We are spirit here and now in a physical body, and not a physical body with a spirit.

'Beyond your physical self, beyond your thoughts and emotions, there lies a realm within you that is pure potential; from this place anything and everything is possible'. [1]

NEW YORK; ITS FRENZIED streets throbbing with the determined footsteps of countless wanderers, reverberating to a mix of endless voices and traffic, casts a spell on visitor and citizen alike. Towering buildings set in seemingly small spaces and with this cacophony of vibrations bouncing off ever maturing walls, the buildings appear to close in, yet empower, with their majesty and strength.

However, to Jim McCloskey, pounding the streets of New York has a special urgency; an excitement tinged with uncertainty, fuelled by a desire, a self-appointed mission, to put wrong to right. For Jim McCloskey is 'The Divine Detective'.

Jim (McCloskey) gave up a successful business career at the age of thirty-seven to enter a seminary, from where he began doing outreach work in a local prison. Called by God to give his life for those unjustly incarcerated, and not even taking time to be ordained, he alone, has been responsible for the freeing of over forty innocent people from America's prisons; men accused of murder, in prison for life.

Now over sixty years old, Jim continues to work alone; following leads, his footwork taking him to many strange places and encounters but, as he says, he doesn't 'stalk' anyone or use any of the usual detective methods, relying strictly on 'intuition' and his own ability. He lives alone, reluctantly admitting that 'yes', it can be a lonely life and at times he feels it would be nice to have someone waiting for him at home; someone to talk to and share the experiences of the day. But then he remembers his 'calling', and the wonderful feeling of knowing he is doing 'God's work'; work in which he feels privileged to be a part; work which brings him personal happiness and satisfaction, seeing innocent people with no hope vindicated, and set free.

And so, in the states, New York, New Jersey and all around that area where he is champion of what were previously thought of as 'lost causes', he is aptly known as 'The Divine Detective'.

When asked how he has alone, managed to achieve so much, he answers simply,

'In the midst of all this darkness, I do lean on God.'

• • •

Ian, Angela Brown's husband, died in 1995. Not long after his passing, Angela and her close friend Jean sat quietly in front of the fire in Angela's home. The fire was a free-standing grate, one with pieces of mock coal piled on top and an electric fan heater underneath. The fan heater gave out a flickering flame effect across the back of the fireplace.

As they sat gazing into the fire, both Angela and Jean were stunned to see the flickering flame turn into the name 'Ian', repeated five or six times; Ian, the name of Angela's dead husband.

• • •

Jim McCloskey entered a seminary in the hope of becoming ordained as a minister. He never realised that ambition. Once he had started doing outreach work (originally as part of his course in the ministry), and feeling the great need of those who had fallen on hard times and who had no one to turn to, he knew that God had called him for a special purpose. From that moment, the moment of his calling, he devoted his entire life to the service of others; and the fact that those 'others' were so called 'convicted killers' whom he believed to be innocent, made his task all the more urgent.

Jim was sure in his faith and 'calling', but what is faith, and what is a calling? A calling, we are told, is being summoned; a vocation, a Divine Call, a sense of fitness for a career or occupation; and faith is the realisation of the expected and confidence in the invisible.

So many of us, and even those who, 'having experienced an experience', still find it difficult to accept that there is more to life than this physical, material side; that there is a 'something else'; that there is more to life than we can 'see 'and 'touch' and 'feel' with our five senses; but what about the sixth sense?

• • •

Josh was only three years old when Smokey, the family cat, died.

Listening to his mother's explanation that Smokey had 'gone to heaven', Josh must have had his own thoughts about that because he was one of those privileged (as many children are, perhaps because of their innocence) to 'see', and so Josh knew that Smokey hadn't gone anywhere! How could he have when he could see him around the house? One day, just as his daddy was about to sit on what had been Smokey's favourite chair, Josh let out a mighty cry: 'Don't! You'll sit on Smokey'; and of course his daddy didn't (sit on the chair); shaken and puzzled, he had to obey.

• • •

So are we getting too 'simplistic' here? – is believing in something more than we can see with our own two eyes, a bit of 'pie in the sky'; over-stretched imagination, an adult 'comfort blanket'? – or is there really the possibility, the probability, of…'something' else?

Trying to avoid words such as 'God' or 'Spirit' (which many are uncomfortable with), is difficult when it seems that evidence points to the fact that we are, each one of us, spirit here and now in a physical body, rather than a physical body with a spirit. Creeping into the very fabric of this worldly life of ours, however, are signs, logos, shouting out to us that the 'other side' (of life), the spirit world, will not be ignored.

A successful greetings card publisher has taken the name 'spirit', as has a cruise ship, while a famous perfume is 'Intuition', and a well-known money exchange agency in London goes by the fabulously original name of 'Holy Ghost'.

A Mind Body and Spirit shop in California, 'Energy Muse', has necklaces for sale with a scroll attached urging the wearer to chant daily, 'I call forth divine protection.' (David Beckham has been photographed wearing the Energy Muse jewellery). A famous English football club, whose supporters are, at the moment, feeling bitter disappointment and despair at the fortunes of the club, have taken heart through hearing that a keen supporter in the Vatican, Rome, has contacted supporters saying he is sending out thoughts (prayers?) for its success. Who would believe it! A moment here perhaps for a smile, and reflection.

Even in business, a newspaper report informs us that; 'Employers are being urged to provide prayer rooms and quiet spaces to meet the needs of employees and promote diversity in the work place.' A guide for employers outlines employers' obligations regarding employees' religious needs – providing prayer rooms, etc. It explains how supporting employees' faiths can make good business sense, helping to attract, motivate and retain staff.

Countries throughout the world continue, in this our twenty-first century, to hold organised prayer groups (sometimes en masse) in times of uncertainty and danger; politicians get together sometimes to pray about issues, and procedures in the House of Commons begin with prayers, while a recent article on the front page of the *Daily Telegraph* has the headline:

'Faith helps believers to rise above the pain'

continuing with; 'Faith in God can relieve pain, according to the results of a scientific experiment carried out by researchers at Oxford University'. Is this perhaps a tentative recognition of the spirit within? (To recognise our spirit as a reality of life; thinking about it *as* life and not necessarily tied up with any religion.)

• • •

Keith, from Cheshire, a professor working at a university in the South of England (and a non-believer), tells what happened when he visited his father's grave. Keith's father died when he was three years old. In October 2006 he had to pass through Runcorn, Cheshire, while on a business trip and remembering that the cemetery where his father was buried was nearby, decided he would make time to visit the grave. He hadn't been there for years, but finally finding the grave, felt sad as he stood helplessly wishing he could do something to tidy it up.

He thought, 'If only I had a carrier bag I could pull up the weeds.' Immediately after the thought – a gust of wind appeared and blew a carrier bag across the churchyard to stick onto the branch of a tree right next to him!

• • •

In thinking about the real you, the real me (our spirit in a physical body), how is it possible for us to discover such truths, such phenomena, for ourselves, each in our own way? There is endless information on the subject, accumulated over centuries, and made available through various establishments, the media, books, lectures, stories, experiences – and sometimes a simple quote says it all;

> 'Just because we can't see all the moon it doesn't mean it's not all there'; and, 'we can't see electricity but…'

Perhaps one of the easiest analogies to help our understanding of spirit (and a spirit world surely most of us would love to believe in), is the analogy of a spinning top. When stationary, we can see well – marked patterns set in vibrant colours; but when the top spins, the colours and patterns disappear, at least from our eyes. The top, in its spinning, has moved onto a different vibration; and so, as we are informed, the spirit world is on a different vibration to ours.

The spirit world, the 'ethereal' world, the 'something else', is there, always, but not visible to our ordinary mortal eyes, so fast, is the (higher) vibration.

Mediums, seers, people who have so called 'second sight' can tune in. They have the gift, and have learnt the 'art' of lifting their own – our own – dense, heavy, earth (material) vibrations on to the higher plane; again, it's all about 'tuning in' to a higher frequency.

The spirit people – those who have passed on to the other side of life, the citizens of heaven, wanting to communicate, learn to help the procedure by lowering their own vibrations (apparently not easy) to link in, tune in, make contact. The same principle seems to apply to healing, and to any other form of communication that seeks to unite the two worlds.

Pam and Brian had travelled the world together (Brian was a Chief Engineer in the Merchant Navy), but it was one incident on a voyage to Greece that they would never forget.

Both sailors and officers had to pass along a passage to get to their duty on watch. On this particular journey, none felt comfortable going along this passage. It didn't matter the time of day or night; or whether they were going to or from their duty on watch; as they made their way to the Bridge, which was set up high and surrounded by glass, they felt uneasy.

One night a young officer on duty saw the face of a very old man, a wrinkled, dark, sun-tanned face, outside the Bridge. It was only when they landed in Greece that the crew learned that the ship had been carrying the body of an old Greek man being returned to his native country.

Only the Captain and the first officer knew of this 'cargo'.

• • •

In considering the possibility of there being a spiritual side to our existence, to our sojourn here on earth, we move in a company that is increasing in numbers every day.

More and more people, and especially young people, saturated with a purely material world are beginning to question and look to the possibility of there being 'another side to life'.

A recent headline in a *Sunday Times* paper had the heading 'God is the new drug of choice for today's young rebels', explaining that there is a genuine thirst among many young people to establish strong moral codes and rules. Referring to themselves as being spiritual, but not religious, giving up alcohol, drug taking and casual sex is synonymous with many of their parents' western culture. (Yet again enforcing the forecast made by wise men decades ago that this century would see a return to spirituality in a big way.)

"People are becoming excited by Christianity again: there are huge crowds. Among the young, what is happening is amazing. There is a hunger for belonging, for believing. There is a hunger and slowly it is being fed."

Words spoken in 2006 by John Sentamu, Archbishop of York, but words that could, apparently, relate to many religions.

• • •

Could this surge, this seemingly 'new seeking', be happening partly because of the crises facing our world today. Such turmoil, uncertainty and anxiety facing us on so many fronts, forcing world leaders to re-think our life style, to work together in the search for a new pathway as they urgently try to head off impending disasters.

Out of the trauma, are we perhaps going to find ourselves again; find our true selves? Oliver James, a leading thinker of today, predicts that 'as our values begin to change, we'll start to feel a lot better'. With other prominent voices echoing his thoughts; 'Not having so much money, material wealth, could be a good thing. Maybe we will have time to think about the deeper things in life, things we haven't thought about before; who are we, why are we here, what are we about, what is it all about?'

(Incidentally, keeping the two minutes silence on Remembrance Day, this November 2008, seemed to be – perhaps more than ever in recent times – especially poignant and deeply thoughtful. Observing the crowds as the cameras panned from street to shopping mall, from church service to Cenotaph, the two minutes silence seemed to show a united, spiritual front; a display of 'togetherness'; a gelling together in reverence and in rededication, portraying the highest and best of what it means to be truly human.)

* * *

My husband had the most beautiful smile. Everyone who knew him commented on it. It was warm and friendly, caring and 'happy'.

One day, some years after his death, I was feeling low and missing him so much that I concentrated on how he had looked, and thought especially of his smile. I wonder, I asked myself, 'Will I ever see that beautiful smile again?' and felt so sad.

That evening, just starting to peel a potato for dinner, I cried out in shock as there, right in front of me, embedded on the skin of the potato was a huge, smiley face; no mistaking it, it was there for all to see proving to me, anyway, that answers can come in many ways, even in the form of a humble vegetable.

* * *

If, as it would appear, we are all first and foremost, spirit, in a physical body, how can we 'feel' this; how can we become aware of this seemingly magical state of being which transforms lives and gives meaning to our very existence?

* * *

During the Second World War, Geoff was stationed in the desert. After spending some money – possibly in the 'mess', he noticed in the change an old penny with a mark, a small indentation, at the temple of the King's head. He again spent money, and noticed that the coin was back in the change, so decided to keep it. He kept it in his breast pocket.

Later on in the war, Geoff was wounded in battle, and the penny saved his life. A 'bullet' ricocheted from off the coin in his pocket, missed his heart, hitting him in the face, on the temple; at the same place as the indentation on the coin.

* * *

It seems to be that, miracles happen every day, but are they recognised? Miracles can happen to you and to me but would we know one if it happened? Would we accept, if we experienced one? Would we stop and think 'yes, such and such was extraordinary, marvellous, amazing!' Maybe the experience, the incident, once registered, would soon be forgotten, anyway; or perhaps it would stay, smouldering, at the back of our minds; or would we ponder deeply on it, trying to understand where this 'phenomenon' had come from and why? (We cannot even imagine the complex forces behind every event that occurs in our lives. There is a conspiracy of coincidences that weaves the web of karma or destiny and creates an individual's personal life – mine, and yours.)[2] Unbelievable as it was, a black man was voted in as President of the United States of America in 2009; it was also 'strange' and 'remarkable' that his convention acceptance speech, a date scheduled long before Barack Obama became the Democratic nominee, took place forty-five years to the day after Martin Luther King's, 'I have a dream' speech.

One of the easiest, and possibly the first road we could travel on to find our own 'miracle', is down the road of 'intuition'. Jim McCloskey, the Divine Detective, tells us that in his work, he relies strictly on 'intuition', and his own ability; but haven't we all, at one time or another, experienced this incredulous phenomena known as 'intuition'…often termed as a 'gut' feeling about something; and how amazed we are when this gut feeling is proved to be right?

(Ferry disaster survivors when interviewed talked of 'being saved' by their 'instinct'. One man said he was surprised to 'have been saved' by his 'instinct' and not by his logic or his brain; another passenger saying she acted purely on her instinct.)

Intuition, when our inner voice talks to us, giving us guidance, answers, when we might have a strange feeling of knowing something we did not know we knew. This 'inner-voice' (is this also the voice of our conscience?).

Dame Kelly Holmes, athlete and Double Olympic Champion in Athens 2004, knows something about spiritual guidance and the help that can come through intuition, assurance, signs inspiring her with confidence, with self-belief.

In her book, *Black, White & Gold*, her autobiography, she tells of being undecided as to whether she should compete in the two events at the Athens Olympics; the 800 metres and the 1500 metres. She sat in the car with two of her friends on her way to her last session on the track before having to decide, when she said – flicking through the radio stations, humming along – 'I'm just in the mood to listen to Tina Turner's "Simply the Best".' To their amazement, just as they drew up at the track, the song started playing. Her friend Zara murmured, 'Oh my God!' but, 'The coincidence gave me goose-bumps; fired me up for my session, the last one before the Olympics.'

Kelly continues; 'I became aware of that same strange feeling that I had experienced before I broke the British record in 1997 and before I won the Olympic bronze in Sydney. I was floating. My body was working perfectly. Nothing could touch me.'

• • •

Family and friends quietly gathered around the coffin of a woman in the front room of her home before the funeral, were startled by a noise coming from the next room. On investigating, they found that a photograph of the dead woman had mysteriously dropped from the wall.

• • •

On arriving in Athens, Kelly Holmes went immediately to her room in the Olympic Village; her first heat was the next day. Settling in and rearranging the room for her own comfort, she opened the door to let in some air. She sat on the bed listening to music, when, 'a gust of cold air blew in round my face. I'm not religious but for that brief moment I felt as if there was something watching over me. It made me feel completely relaxed. I knew I was ready,' and so she was.

· · ·

Intuition; a mysterious, hidden instinct that appears as a thought, a dream, a sudden 'knowing' of what to do; maybe in a case of indecision, a sudden change of plan. Perhaps a change of travel plans that result in avoiding a nasty incident; but surely we have all, at one time or another, felt this 'urge', this call to do something differently to what has been previously arranged, changing things, often acting in 'blind faith'?

Albert Einstein, scientist, is quoted as saying; 'The only real valuable thing is intuition', and successful business people such as Bill Gates, Jack Welch, Donald Trump and Oprah Winfrey, have all pointed to intuition as a major factor in their business success. Oprah is especially open about her use of intuition in daily life and states her 'mission' is; "I want people to see things on our show that makes them think differently about their lives...to be a light for people. To make a difference...to open their minds and see things differently...how to get in touch with the spiritual part of their life."

· · ·

For some unexplained reason, a year or two after my husband died I began to have photographs of him sent to me by friends, and even a stranger, who got in touch with someone I knew and through him sent me a school photograph of my husband. It has happened at least four times and left me most surprised (and delighted of course), and eagerly awaiting the next one.

· · ·

Intuition; only one of the many ways in which our 'inner voice' can resonate with us; separating, by-passing the distractions of the physical in a miraculous 'surge' that makes us 'know'; be 'aware', 'feel', 'sense'. The 'inner voice' which of course, when heeded, can lead us onto the 'inner way' (the inner being the motivator of the outer, physical self), but what *is* the inner way?

The inner way is that which takes us through our dreams, our emotions; our responses, our intellect; motivating our very being; fuelling our thoughts, directing our actions, and of course, the inner way is the way of our potential spirituality – which makes us what we are.

Now that we are here, together, at this point (and we must be if you are still with me, reading these words), it is time for you, if you will, to make your own contribution to this book. Time, if you will, to sit back and recall your own moment or moments of intuition. Remembering that it could be a so-called 'coincidence' that made you sit up and take notice, leading on from there to an answer or resolution of something worrying, wonderful, surprising.

At the back of the book there are a number of blank pages. Having decided what was your own 'experience' or 'experiences' of intuition, start writing! You may start with only a few words, a date perhaps, a sentence, then, discovering that your intuition has more about it than you had ever imagined possible, go on, write it all down, and insert your own extra pages if necessary. Continue writing as we move further on, making your own notes, your own observations, recording your own experiences, which I am sure you will evidence in time, if you haven't already done so.

Our inner journey, our inner way, has really taken off when we have reached the stage of, *seriously*, 'thinking about it', because once we have had, even a glimmer, of the possibilities inherent in our spiritual nature, the interest, the 'call', will never go away.

Cropping up from time to time, with maybe even years in between, lying, as we might think, 'dormant', it will return to give us, strange as it may seem, 'food for thought'; undeniable proof that there is, indeed, incredible as it may seem, a plan, a reason, and life will never be the same again!

• • •

Jane, from Somerset, tells us about buying a tiny Siamese kitten. She watched as it played in the snow, then, picking it up, said, 'Oh, your tiny paws are frozen'. Going indoors, the radio started to play the song from the opera, *La Boheme*, 'Your tiny hand is frozen', and so she named the kitten Mimi, the character in the song. She had Mimi for twenty-three years. Weeks after Mimi died, still thinking about her, she chose another Siamese kitten. As she strapped her basket into the car to take her home, the car radio played, 'Your tiny hand is frozen', from *La Boheme*. Jane accepted it as being from Mimi, from the other side of life, giving her approval to the new kitten, which she also named Mimi.

• • •

To go further in trying to understand, to know our true selves, our spirit, the real you, the real me, a richer, fuller side to our existence other than this material world we inhabit (a writer has said; 'We are spiritual beings in a physical body and the greatest enemy to understanding this is materialism.'), we need to go back to a previous page and think about the question; 'If we are all, as it would appear, spirit in a physical body, how can we "feel" this, how can we know? Having now a little understanding of 'spirit' as existing on a different plane, a different, higher, lighter vibration to our own, heavy, dense material vibration, we need now to go into the 'silence', sitting alone, quietly and comfortably, in contemplative mood – as if preparing for a time of 'meditation'.

As you sit there, look at your hands. Study them carefully.

Take your time. Study them and think about what makes them different from other hands. Perhaps you will come to the understanding that 'hands are hands', except some are fatter or shorter or female or male hands, and so on; but, after all, 'hands are hands'. Touch your face and have the same sense of understanding, that other 'faces are faces'; touch your hair and think in the same way. A famous surgeon who developed heart by-pass surgery has said that it didn't matter who the people (patients) were – celebrity or others – 'once you were inside the skin, they are all more or less the same'; so what makes us different?

This reminds me of a group of young soldiers – eighteen-year-olds – I shared a train corridor with a few years ago. They were enthralled in a conversation about Reiki Healing they had experienced at their camp. So enthusiastic were they that they included me in their conversation, trying hard to impress on me the power of Reiki. The conversation turned to other, so-called, paranormal topics, and then, the most outspoken of them, the tallest and probably their 'leader', looking directly at me, pinched his arm, saying, 'I'll tell you what, there's more to life than just this!'

So what makes us different? Our 'spirit', which is the motivating factor in our lives, is that which makes us what we are. We go hither and thither experiencing the highs and lows of life as on a never-ending carousel; a persona; a person, a spirit, the real me, the one and only you! So what makes us different? Our spirit, the motivating factor in our lives, which makes us what we are, is also that which makes us different.

• • •

A man gave a talk about his life as a Benedictine Monk living in a monastery for seven and a half years. Then, he told how, one Wednesday night, he heard a voice in his head that simply said,

'Go home.' He tried to ignore it but, during the following seven services (worship, held every day), the same words, 'go home', were repeated over and over. Finally, he told the Brother Superior about it and that he would be leaving on the Saturday; which he did. Leaving with only the habit he wore, no money, no possessions, he hitch-hiked his way home to the north of England where he still lives today; still serving God, but in a different way.

• • •

To find our own spirituality is not necessarily being religious; but to send out a sincere, heartfelt feeling of concern or love, or to care for someone, or some creature or plant – or any living thing – to be sensitive to the needs, the suffering of others; love, care, concern, this is our spiritual side shining through. It seems to be, however, that in having 'altruistic' feelings, we don't always associate them with the word 'spiritual'. And yet we all recognise the expression 'he has a good heart, a good spirit'; 'he will be able to rise above the tragic circumstances'; to rise above meaning 'the right spirit'; 'it was her spirit that kept her going, against all the odds'. We may have the vocabulary, but do we really have the understanding of the word 'spiritual', and have we accepted that we are all spirit, here and now, in a physical body?

Do we realise the strength of our feelings, our moods, to direct and control our lives? Feelings, emotions, emanating from the deep well of the inner-self, a vital part of our spirit, making us who we are; and if you can't, at this moment, accept the major role that your feelings, your emotions, have played in your life, just sit back, and think about it.

• • •

Fay finished making the bed and left the room for a while, on returning, to find, to her astonishment, two one pound coins lying in the centre (of the bed). As she stood, bewildered, staring at the coins, her six-year-old daughter who was in another room (and had not been in Fay's room), suddenly called out; 'Mam can you remember when Uncle George used to give me and Sam a pound each?' Sam is her brother, and Uncle George gave them each a pound every time he saw them. Unable to contain herself with wonder at all this, she decided to phone her husband at work and tell him the tale. She got through to him and after telling him, said, 'Isn't it strange'? 'Yes,' he answered, 'and isn't it strange that I am here now, standing at Uncle George's grave?'

• • •

Remember when you were looking forward to a certain social event, a party, maybe a family reunion, a small gathering, a large formal affair; you arrived there in a good, happy mood but something changed everything; something that made you feel annoyed, or unwelcome, or even sad. Perhaps you couldn't understand your sudden change of mood, and never did understand it, but it happened; and vice versa, you go to an event not particularly looking forward to it, and it turns out to be one of the best times in your life.

These experiences, occasions, you (and me), with feelings, emotions, 'ablaze', living the life; when our spiritual nature is in the forefront of the action, telling us something, telling us that – which the purely physical never could.

Feelings, emotions, signs; we can liken life to a paper chase, looking for clues as we travel along, ever trying to guide ourselves to the best; but is 'the best' not already present, within us, unrecognised? Unrecognised until we start to lean on our spiritual nature; 'tune in', listen to the inner voice; tap into what is, and has always been, our true potential.

When difficulties, worries, sadness come along, have you ever noticed that just as life appears to be at its worst – to quote Marty, a good Irish Catholic friend of mine, 'something always seems to turn up'? Something turns up to 'lighten the load', 'put a spark of brightness' into an otherwise desperate situation. Can you look back and recall such a time? A bad situation you experienced but was there not an incident, perhaps an 'occurrence', that pierced even this deepest of black, tingeing it with a calmer tone, a softer hue. A letter, an unexpected phone call, a vivid dream, a stranger; it could be anything; but in that 'anything' which in itself came along 'out of the blue', you saw hope; you were uplifted; you were able to carry on.

Since the beginning of time people of all ages and from all walks of life have been sustained by a belief in what transcends the everyday; by this 'irresistible' part of us; our spiritual nature. An irresistible something that is always there, beckoning us on; trying to impress on us – perhaps in the humblest or in the most ingenious of ways – to look to our spiritual self.

• • •

One day, as Mary took her grandson Stan aged four, out for their walk as usual, he suddenly said, 'Granddad's in the house.' (But Granddad Bill was at sea, an engineer in the Merchant Navy.) And just as Stan insisted his granddad was at home, so did Mary, his grandmother, equally insist that he was at sea. Then Stan came out with, 'He's at home and he's got something white on his arm.'

The walk over, they returned to their street to find a neighbour waiting for them. The neighbour told Mary that her husband was back at home, and she didn't want her to get a shock going into the house to find him there when he should have been at sea. She also told Mary that he had broken his arm, and that was why he had had to return home. True enough, when Mary and Stan walked into the house, there was Granddad Bill waiting for them – with a broken arm; (hence the white, the little lad her grandson had seen.)

• • •

The stream of life as it charges (or trickles) along, poses a never-ending series of questions to answer, decisions to make, problems to solve, all entwined in a day in a life, or should we say a life in a day, because that is what it can often seem.

Observing people making their way to work or college or wherever in the morning, observing them and wondering what sort of day will they face? What circumstances will they find themselves in? Who will they meet? How will they react to whatever the day may bring? For it is often out of the simplest incidents that big issues arise.

How do we react to an encounter with an unpleasant or perhaps impatient shop assistant, or some other worker in public...to any stranger we may come in contact with? To be spiritual would be to try to understand that the unpleasantness, the impatience, could be a result of the worry, the stress, going on in their own lives as they struggle to conceal all problems and carry on with their daily tasks. Just to stop and think; give a little care, a little understanding to what another might be facing or feeling; might be going through at that particular moment, can often diffuse a situation that could perhaps lead to, if not checked, a confrontation.

To stop and think, have a care, a concern for another; and here we must include the animal kingdom. How many of us appreciate the fact that an animal may also be having a bad day? – that it may be feeling unwell, not want to be bothered or pushed or pulled around, or handled.

Care, love, concern, all coming under the heading 'spiritual'; and what matter if these spiritual thoughts and feelings are perhaps, as we might think, misdirected, misunderstood or rebuffed? What does matter is that a positive or kind thought will never ever, go astray.

• • •

Anthony Trevor was a natural psychic. From the age of seven he could see spirit people, and throughout his long life he accepted that he could see things that a lot of other people couldn't; he could see the spirit world almost everywhere, but on one occasion, he was 'flabbergasted', as he said at the time. He was standing at the bar of the Bull and Bush in Hampstead Heath, London, when a man dressed as a highwayman rushed in. The figure strode to the bar and banged on the counter with his fist, and of course the barman, who couldn't see him anyway, ignored him, so the stranger grabbed his pistol, shot at the barman and disappeared![3]

• • •

Bernard D'espagnat, an eighty-seven-year-old old French physicist and philosopher, has won the 2009 prestigious Templeton Prize, said to be the world's largest annual award to an individual, for his work affirming the spiritual dimension of life. D'espagnat, it is said, has 'explored the unlimited, the openings that new scientific discoveries offer in pure knowledge, and in questions that go to the very heart of our existence and humanity'. The report continues, 'New discoveries indicate a reality beyond the reach of science but human intuitions in art, music and spirituality can bring us closer to this ultimate reality.' Science, swathed as it is in academia, and within its own artificial setting, cannot capture the 'truth' of the moment. Perhaps the genius of the musician, the artist, the writer, soaring to great heights in a flow of creativity come close, feeling their inspiration to be as 'not of this world.[4] But it is so mysterious that we cannot know or even imagine it.'

D'espagnat continues, 'I believe we ultimately come from a superior entity to which awe and respect is due, and which we should not try to approach by trying to conceptualise too much.' He said, 'It's more a question of feeling.' D'espagnat goes on to claim that the intuitions people have when moved by great art or spiritual beliefs help them to grasp a bit more of ultimate reality.[5]

The intuitions people have when moved by great art or spiritual beliefs! Intuition; the feeling, the inner knowledge we all have access to and perhaps the easiest, the most easily available 'miracle' we all have access too, but so often unrecognised, ignored.

Intuition, when our inner voice talks to us giving us guidance, answers; when we have a strange feeling of knowing something we did not know we knew – Jim McCloskey the Divine Detective relying strictly on intuition…seeing coincidences as meaningful life opportunities…

Many people believe that there is no such thing as a coincidence (as in the dictionary definition of the word – that a coincidence is a concurrence of events or circumstances without apparent causal connection); but that coincidences happen to tell us something, have a reason, give us a 'message'. There is an old saying; 'A coincidence is God's way of performing a miracle anonymously.'

'You just don't know what you would have done if, say, a certain thing had (or had not) happened; it was incredible the way everything worked out.' 'Your car breaks down at the side of a deserted road, and just when you have resigned yourself to 'being stranded' for hours, a tow truck comes along.' 'Meeting up with a certain person again after many years was unbelievable and completely changed your life!'

Coincidences can set a pattern of thought so often igniting intuition, leading us on, making us, often by the sheer dramatic input of the experience, stop! Hold our breath! In – awe – of a something we have not seen, or touched, or have even physically 'heard'…but have surely 'felt'.

• • •

21

My name is Ray Kennedy and in 1958, although in the army, I was serving my second term of duty on board ship off Christmas Island, working as a stevedore. The work was tough, loading and unloading supplies. We unloaded everything you could think of, including cargoes that contained everything to build roads, airfield and runway; fuel was also needed.

I was lucky enough to go on leave to Honolulu and it was there that an episode happened in my life that I would like to tell you about. I went swimming off Waikiki beach and found myself in difficulties. On going under for the fourth time, a man swathed in white bandages held me up. He held me until a lifeguard came on his surfboard and took me back to shore.

On thanking the lifeguard, I also wanted to thank the man in the white bandages, but was told there was no one else there! For years I did not even wonder why someone in bandages would go into the water, after all, would they not drag him under?

Now my wife believes it must have been a 'guardian angel' and so has been delving into the folklore of Hawaii. The nearest we can find is the Goddess Pelle whom, it is said, comes to peoples' aid dressed in white robes! I wonder![6]

• • •

We none of us know 'every which way' life will turn for us, whether we are nine or ninety-nine, but the fact remains that we will all, surely, at one time or another, have experienced the phenomenon known as coincidence, intuition, déjà vu and the like. Often in everyday experiences our inner self, our 'spirit', guides us, helps us; when we have the 'feel good' factor, that wondrous unexplainable result of touching on the inner way, blending with the other side of life; accepting that we are spirit in a physical body; thus discovering the 'true self'.

Life; in all its dexterity, its moods, its cunning, gives us the opportunity to make the most of the great, full, enriched person we can become…life…the inner way…happiness… opportunity …fulfilment…life…

• • •

Isabella Macleod who owns a second-hand bookshop in Inverness-shire has had many strange experiences, from childhood: unusual occurrences, that seem to have 'followed her', from time to time. Not so long ago, a man phoned her bookshop asking for a specific book on old motor bikes; she could tell that he really wanted this particular book and she knew that she had it! After a thorough search, however, she couldn't find it.

Three months later while busy moving and checking stock she found the book under a big pile; picking it up, she told her husband about the man and felt sorry that she had no way of contacting him to tell him of her find, remembering how keen he had been to have it.

One hour later, the man phoned.

• • •

Twelve years ago, Isabella had a strange, unnerving experience that shook her rigid. She still talks about it today, and probably always will, as she remembers every detail, every little move, every word, and is still as puzzled as she was then by the meaning of it all.

Was she the 'absent presence' in a – what proved to be world news headline – tragedy? Was it, was there, proof that she had somehow slipped into another dimension; not a time dimension, as part of her experience was, terrifyingly, happening parallel to the tragedy. Her experience was as extraordinary as it was frightening, as moving as it was unexplainable and Isabella would love some answers as to whatever happened to her on the night of 30th August 1997. Can you recall the significance of that date? – when Isabella went to bed late, as usual, in an ordinary frame of mind, and woke up to find herself faced with some unknown, chilling, reality.

The phenomenon we are talking about here is the vitally important 'dream state'; but with Isabella it was more than a dream, perhaps more than a vision; a surreal experience where she tapped into a something, a life, of which she had previously no part, either by thought or word. The experience has now become her biggest personal problem to solve, her enigma.

With Isabella's story unfolding in the next chapter, we move into another part of our spirituality, a part that no one can deny, the time for sleep. The time for sleep, when we might gravitate into the dream state, from where it is possible to receive advice, help, messages, from the other side of life; day dreams from which we might find inspiration; cat naps to revitalise the physical, and visions which have a reality all their own.

Chapter Two

Understanding the inner-self

> During all human history there has been a belief, not confined
> to any one country or creed or level of culture, that mankind,
> or at least some men and women, had other means of
> perception and of acquiring knowledge than the five senses,
> and were able to get in touch with modes of existence
> unfamiliar to everyday experience. The universal prevalence
> of stories of ghosts and haunted houses, of second sight and
> dreams that come true is evidence of this belief.[1]

30TH AUGUST 1997 AND Isabella Macleod made her way to
bed late as usual and fell into a deep sleep; a sleep that was to
turn into a vision – or was it some other reality?

Isabella had a dream (or whatever it was), and in the dream
she was travelling down a river, but on reflection, insisted the
river was more like a canal except that it had stately homes along
each side. Troubled about calling it a river or a canal (she couldn't
say why), she finally described it as simply 'water', with stately
homes lining the bank along each side.

Travelling along in a boat (Isabella couldn't describe the type
of boat), it then seemed to veer to the side and bump into a little
fair-haired girl who was standing at the water's edge. The boat,

then hastily pushed into the side, revealed that the little girl had disappeared and the adult Princess Diana was standing in her place.

The Princess was beautifully 'made up', everything about her appearance, her hair, make-up, all blending in with the peach suit she was wearing. As Isabella saw Diana, she was also aware of a huge building behind her, with a heavy studded door. The Princess, probably noticing the puzzled expression on Isabella's face said, 'It's all right, come with me,' and turned to walk towards the building. Hesitant, Isabella followed her. She followed the Princess and on entering this 'stately home' was amazed to find the place empty.

With bare, dark brown polished wood floors and nothing else, it had such a barren, cold feel about it that Isabella had to exclaim, 'Is this where you live? It's so cold and empty!' 'Yes,' Diana replied, and again, 'Come with me.'

Now Isabella noticed at one side of the hall a huge staircase, straight and beautifully designed, fitted with a rich-looking crimson carpet. She followed Diana up the stairs until, at the top they looked into an elegant, bright, colourful room, full of warmth. Isabella remained standing at the top of the stairs staring into this most magnificent, yet inviting of rooms; Diana moved further in to stand at the other side of the room, directly opposite, in front of an alcove, rounded at the top.

Beside Isabella, a big clock with four faces stood on a table. She noticed the time on it read 4 o'clock. At this same moment, Diana lifted her hand in a gesture of farewell saying, 'I must go,' backed out of the alcove and disappeared.

As Diana disappeared, Isabella felt 'shaken' and irritated by the sound of bells ringing, finally realising, in a disturbing way, that it was her phone.

Trying hard to pull herself together, not seeming to be able to 'get out of' this 'thing' she was in – this reality that was hers

– but not hers; true, and as real as any other encounter in ordinary, daily life, yet so unimaginable that how could it be true...? The phone kept ringing; somehow becoming aware that it was very early in the morning, she struggled to answer it.

The excited yet anguished tone in her friend's voice told her that something awful had happened. 'Have you heard the news? The Princess of Wales has been killed in a car accident.' Still in a state of confusion as to what she had experienced and now struggling with the belief of it all, with everything, even to the validity of this phone call, she was completely devastated as her friend continued; 'Diana was pronounced dead at four o'clock this morning.'

Seven years later, Isabella and two American friends visited Kensington Palace, and as they strolled around, enjoying the history and splendour of the place, her friend Pat suddenly called out, 'Look Isabella, there's the clock with the four faces, and there's the staircase with the crimson carpet.'

Over the years, many people have heard the story of Isabella's vision, and she has gradually come to wonder if the water she travelled on (not wanting to call it a river or a canal) could have been to symbolise the lake at Althorp – beside which Diana was later buried.

Having checked with the estate agent, there is indeed a big heavy studded door such as the one Isabella described, at the main entrance; a gate house door, very prominent, around six feet in height. And Isabella also wonders at the awful, cold feeling she had as her first impression of the place, and wonders if it could have been to symbolise Diana's unhappiness there as a child.

Isabella has assured me that the reality, the intenseness of her experience, has not left her over the years, nor has it been added to in any way.

• • •

Worrying about Janice, a close friend who lived near Perth, Scotland, and who I knew had a lot of problems – including health ones, and wondering if there was anything I could do to help her, I took my usual afternoon walk. I wondered if maybe I was exaggerating a difficult situation with Janice; getting it out of proportion, not knowing the full story.

Nearly home, a plain white van appeared on the main road and, crossing over, passed in front of me along a side road. There, on the side of the van, in bold, large letters, was a name neither I nor my friends have seen before in this area (of England). 'Ian Campbell', the name of my friend's dead husband.

With that, I hurried home feeling quite perturbed by the experience, made a few enquiries to Scotland, a few phone calls that set in motion a series of events much needed for Janice, who tragically passed away not long after.

• • •

Isabella's dream poses some questions. She was asleep in her bed at the time of the accident, but is it possible, could she, in some sensationally strange way, have linked, subconsciously, into another vibration...had she entered another dimension, one perhaps running parallel to our own?

Everything about the dream/vision was so real to Isabella, and with the evidence at the end of the experience, that she had indeed linked into, perhaps a tiny part of this tragedy as it was unfolding, it is surely unique.

Why did the princess suddenly decide it was 'time to go'; and why did she 'go' just as the clock struck four, at the time the accident was announced by the media to the world? Could the 'water' Isabella was worried about describing have symbolised the lake at Althorp; the cold, empty house with the barren feel about it symbolise Diana's unhappy childhood spent at Althorp; and why did this mysterious 'vision' happen to Isabella?! She does say that since childhood she has had experiences where she has predicted future events.

. . .

In the past few years, we have heard of and seen on television, the artist who paints the future. Accidents, terrorist attacks, appear to him before they happen, while he sleeps. Immediately he awakes, he sets them down while still vividly etched in his mind.

Amy was only eleven years old when, a few months before the 9/11 attack on New York, she had a dream in which she was standing with her granny, high up in one of two huge buildings standing next to each other (she now knows they were the twin towers). They were looking at the identical building next to them and saw a plane fly into it; later, from outside they watched as fire fighters pulled people from the debris.

More recently, Amy dreamt of another terrorist attack before it happened and told people about it, the attack in Mumbai on the Taj Mahal Hotel; (she didn't know the name at the time but gave the exact description), with smoke coming out of the windows and the big blast in the wall where the attack happened. In the dream, Amy was one of the onlookers outside when it happened, filming the tragedy.

Bill, a window cleaner, saw Concord crash into flames as it left the runway, clearly, and with all the detail surrounding it, in a dream the night before it happened.

(We take it for granted that we live in a 'solid' world of space and time, advancing from moment to moment according to unchangeable laws, and that we are stuck in the place where we happen to be 'at the moment'. We are, in a sense, 'trapped'. We feel this particularly strongly when we are bored or miserable – that we are helplessly at the mercy of this physical world into which we happen to have been born. Yet these odd experiences all seem to show that this is untrue. The 'real you' is not trapped in space and time. With a certain kind of effort of will it can rise above space and time, and be 'elsewhere'.)[2]

It seems that there is little doubt, and to those who have experienced such phenomena, no doubt at all, that there is a state we can reach, whether in the cold light of day or in the dark shades of night, where we can be part of another reality. For perhaps most people, however, just to be able to remember our dreams, and any advice or messages we receive through them, is wonder enough. Sarah, a practitioner of Shamanic Healing, does not worry about any writing she may have to do for papers or magazines or books; she has the confidence to know that her inspiration will come to her while she sleeps, waking in the morning to put down on paper what she has been given.

• • •

When Maria left her home in Hungary to come and live in England, she was so sad as she had to leave her pet dog Gombi behind, but she knew that he was safe with her mother.

Recently, in 2008, Gombi, by now aged fourteen years, became ill and had to be put to sleep. Gombi died on a Saturday. The next day, Sunday, Maria saw a black and white shadow in the bathroom but did not know at that time that her dog had died; her mother phoned her later to tell her.

Days later, when again she was in the bathroom, she felt something brush against her leg and knew that it was Gombi, as it was a habit of his to follow her whenever she went into the bathroom.

• • •

Travelling in the sleep state, when the spirit body leaves the physical body, yet is still connected to it by a 'silver cord', [3] is perhaps a common enough occurrence, but not all of us remember, or care to remember, when it happens. Sometimes called 'astral travelling', or an out of body experience (OBE), it can provide proof, wonderful evidence, of the reality of the sleep state, the significance of our dreams. Relating to an OBE or NDE – (near death experience, could it be that the mind is extended more than we realise?) Iris Wilding gives a fascinating account of an adventure she had while astral travelling, having an OBE when she visited a zoo.

While asleep one night, Iris left her body and was transported to a zoo, where a huge gorilla was on the loose, rampaging among crowds of people. Terrified, the screaming crowds scattered hither and thither, desperate to keep out of the path of the raging animal; but Iris somehow felt safe, knowing he couldn't see her in her spirit body.

The next morning, she switched on the TV, to see, on a news programme, people running all over the place screaming, terrified. A gorilla had escaped from a zoo, in California.

• • •

One Thursday night, many years ago, a man had a dream in which he saw an acquaintance of his, William, thrown from his horse, and saw him lying on the ground with blood streaming from his face, which had severe cuts on it. William mentioned his dream to someone the next morning, but being a real 'disbeliever' in such 'things', he could not understand why it made such a strong impression on him. So strongly did he feel about the dream that on the Saturday, he called at William's house to find that he was in bed suffering from bad facial injuries, caused by having been thrown from his horse the day before.

• • •

To return to the present day; David is a young man whose strange dreams have given him cause to think seriously about life; life

31

and death, what is it all about; why are we here; morals and principles; in other words, philosophy.

• • •

Always close to his grandmother, who had practically brought him up, her death was a hard blow to this very sensitive and caring young man. They used to meet regularly in a local cafe for a cup of tea and a chat, and so for David to dream one night that they were doing this was understandable. What was not understandable to David, however, was the fact that he, David, throughout this meeting with his grandmother in the dream state (knowing that she had died), had the uncomfortable 'sense' that "she should not be here"! Is this a remarkable example of while living, fully and consciously, a dream reality, at the same time being also aware that the person with you has 'crossed boundaries' to be there?

• • •

A woman, aged sixty-four years, had reported to doctors at Geneva University Hospital the presence of a pale, translucent third arm.

The woman's neurologist, Asaid Khateb, after examining the case, said the rare phenomenon was 'credible'. 'Swissinfo' reported that the arm appeared to the woman a few days after having a stroke. She does not always perceive the arm, but uses it when it is needed.

Often patients who have had amputations experience sensation or pain where the limb used to be. This can also apply to patients who have had a stroke.

The experience is known as having a 'supernumerary phantom limb' (SPL), but there are only nine known cases of a patient both feeling and seeing an arm that does not exist.

Examinations of the brain using magnetic resonance imaging

(MRI) showed that the Swiss woman actually experienced what she described. [4]

• • •

David, who had the dream about his grandmother, was only eight years old when he had a nightmare of a vision that was to turn into a true situation, five years later.

Dreaming, and in the dream having an OBE (out of body) experience, David found himself at house-top height, looking down on his body as it lay, full stretch, across his own front doorstep, unclothed and with a gaping hole in the back of his neck. Now, years later, he can describe the hole as an 'open wound'.

At age thirteen, suffering from headaches, balance problems, loss of sensation in his body, trapped nerves, he had to have major surgery to remove a tumour attached to his spinal cord (there from birth), growing inside the vertebrae. He remembers hearing that the consultant didn't have much hope of him pulling through.

David was in hospital for three months, completely 'paralysed', and with more operations later, leaving him with a hole in the back of his neck. It was a long time after when, remembering the dream, all he could say about it was, 'How bizarre!'

• • •

While David, in his dream about his grandmother, had the uncomfortable sense at the back of his mind that 'she shouldn't be here', in another dream, three women knew that their loved one had returned from the other side of life, to comfort them. Deepak Chopra, famous author/philosopher, tells us of their experience.

'Tom passed when he was only twenty-two with a brain tumour. His mother was staying at his home the day he passed, along with his sister and his new wife. Tom's passing was peaceful, and that evening the three women stayed up late talking about him. 'We must have talked too late, because we fell asleep in front of the fire,' his mother told Chopra. The next morning, Tom's wife, excited, told them that he had come to her in a dream and reassured her that he was all right. His sister blurted out that Tom had also come to her in a dream saying the same thing; and yes, his mother had the same dream. They all agreed that Tom was so vividly present that it had not seemed like a dream – it was really him.[5]

• • •

A mother told of the time just before her young son died. She was sitting on the bed beside her seven-year-old son who was about to pass when he said to her, 'I can see an angel,' following that up with, 'No, I can see two.'[6]

• • •

For those of us who cannot even begin to imagine how our spiritual side (spiritual nature) can make itsself known to us; who cannot accept intuition and dreams and coincidence as anything other than intuition, dreams, and coincidence, the subtlety of so much that comes from the 'spirit world' (the other side of life, from the 'something else', from 'God') can be both amazing and unbelievable. Lesser, yet still hair-raising incidents occur all the time – but not to Joan! Joan, steady, practical and sensible, not given to imagining things, could often be heard to say, 'I don't have any strange experiences happen to me,' until one day...

Joan and her husband Alan went out for a long drive in the country, stopping at a few places en route before making their way home. Driving back at a leisurely pace, as they neared home, Joan noticed a couple walking along a country path in the opposite direction and soon realised it was their friends Edna and Bob; she mentioned this to Alan who was driving.

Miles further on, they stopped at a car park to watch swans on a lake, a popular spot, got out of their car and as they got out looked at the car parked next to them, and in it sat Edna and Bob; (they were already there when Joan and Alan arrived).

Astounded, Joan asked them, 'Have you just walked along from such and such a place?' 'No, this is as far as we've got, we've just driven here from home,' the couple adamant that they had been no further than the lakeside car park. Joan (to herself anyway) was equally adamant, knowing that she had seen them walking along the road, and still believing it today.

• • •

An art class in progress; the teacher asked the class to help him with a commission he was working on, an oil painting of a typical street scene in New Orleans. Tossing ideas around, the class came up with a street festooned with flowers, houses with high, wrought-iron balconies; a port, a paddle steamer on a river; negro bands marching with brilliantly clad dancers twirling around. The artist, painting as they talked, soon came up with an excellent portrayal of their ideas.

A day or two later, Pat, a member of the class, was stunned to receive a postcard from her brother of the same scene – the street with flowers, houses with high wrought-iron balconies, the port, the bands, the dancers, all identical with the painting the class had helped to produce. Pat's brother John was a musician on a cruise ship that had called at New Orleans, hence the postcard. The following week she took it to the class to show the others, who were equally stunned, all agreeing it was 'uncanny'.

Not long after, Pat received the tragic news that her brother, John, the musician, aged forty, had died suddenly of a heart attack.

Strange, but true, incidents that happen in life all the time, giving us pause for thought.

In his television programme *Around the World in 80 Faiths*, Sussex vicar Peter Owen Jones, talked of his hope to understand the depth of humanity's fascination with the divine; his goal being to 'take the religious pulse of the planet'. The vicar commenting that he felt rewarded with the evidence that religion is, to quote, 'alive and kicking'; but perhaps evidence points to the fact that the key words are not so much those with 'a religious context', as those that speak about a revival, a belief in what 'transcends the everyday'. Here we have – as we have already been reading about, often in ordinary, everyday incidents, *because of some strange intervention* – (is it a 'wake up' call?), something that makes us 'sit up', take notice, 'think', ponder.

Joan, supposedly not seeing the two friends she knew that she *had* seen. Brian, in an out of body experience, seeing himself lying prostrate across the doorstep of his home with a hole in the back of his neck, a preview of what was to come! The mother comforted and assured by the words of her dying son 'I can see two angels'; Maria, physically 'feeling' the brush of her pet dog Gombi against her legs days after she heard that he had died; and Isabella, her curious, yet 'telling' dream/vision, giving us so much to think about. Potential life-changing events; perhaps not in the usual, dramatic way, but 'could be' life-changing, all the same.

• • •

Henry Ziegland, a Texan, led a quiet, uneventful life until one day in 1893 he decided he no longer wanted to marry his fiancée.

Distraught by the news, she committed suicide.

Her brother, devastated by the turn of events, sought out Ziegland and shot him. He then turned the pistol on himself and died instantly.

Ziegland, however, survived, the bullet simply grazing his face, dazing him, before embedding itself into a tree. Twenty years later, Ziegland decided to cut down the bullet-marked tree, but it had grown so huge that he had to blast it out of the ground with dynamite. The explosion sent the old bullet flying through the air and straight through his skull, killing him in seconds. Twenty years late, the bullet found its mark.

• • •

Ancient civilisations were aware of, and accepted as natural, all the phenomena many of us now regard as supernatural. They knew the power of 'healing', the power of 'thought'; they took notice of omens, signs, dreams, seeing messages from the spirit world in many everyday events, these messages often coming through their ancestors, whom they revered. They knew how to unlock priceless knowledge from life itself. They knew how to be 'in tune' with their 'spiritual' self, how to 'connect', knowing themselves to be much greater than the small, physical space they inhabited on the earth plane; and not bowed down by the shackles of the material world we now live in, ancient civilisations saw themselves as an integral part of the bigger picture; the Universe.

Red Indians – every tribe is different but they have many things in common – do not believe that their religion is a group effort but rather an individual 'walk', their 'path', sometimes referred to as the 'Medicine Way', which is personal to them and their creator. They tend to listen to the inner voice of spirit as opposed to written scriptures or spiritual supervisors. They believe that 'this' life we live in is merely a 'school' in which we learn life's lessons, after which they will pass on to the 'Happy Hunting Ground' or 'Spirit World' where they will be with their ancestors.

They believe very much in 'walking a good walk' in this life; be good to your fellow man, respect 'Mother Earth', be true to yourself; act with character, courage and dignity.

Thinking back to our understanding of the spirit world as being on a higher vibration to our earth plane, remember the analogy of a spinning top – when stationary, we can see the colourful, well-marked patterns, but when the top spins, the colours and patterns disappear; the top, in its spinning moving on to a higher vibration).

Penny Peirce, in her book *Frequency*, tells us; 'Everything is vibrating energy, and each of us has a personal vibration – a frequency of energy held moment by moment in our spirit, thoughts, emotions, and body – that communicates who we are to the world and helps shape our reality.'[7]

We have already touched on how, in an extreme emotion, we are transported into another state of being, a state of heightened awareness where we see (and feel) things differently...perhaps in a time of great joy, or despair, when we touch on something that is not the 'norm'. (Terry Waite, former Beirut hostage, talks about himself and the other hostages as being in a state of heightened awareness during their years of captivity.)

• • •

Rachel, a holiday representative working in Mexico, will never forget the night, walking back home after a day's work, seeing a family standing at the cross roads ahead of her; 'a bald-headed man with a child on his back and other children around him. He wore what looked like a robe made of hessian tied in the middle with a rope. The little family crossed the road in front of me and just disappeared. I was so amazed I looked all over for them, this way and that, but they had completely disappeared.' She herself claims, 'It was as natural as if there are spirit people there all the time, around us, but suddenly an infra red light comes on enabling us to see them – "to tune in".' Rachel wonders if she was able to 'see' things, to see into another dimension, because she was in a susceptible state at the time, having heart-ache, due to a broken romance.

Rita is a woman who talks quite knowingly on vibrations, radio waves, frequency and so on, and would understand what Rachel was saying about an 'infra red light' coming on and so able to actually 'see' spirit people. We sat talking one day and the conversation turned to 'the other side' (of life). As Rita put it, 'energy waves, pulsations, unseen energies, other dimensions, are playing around us all the time; *there could be a spirit street, right here, running along between us, with spirit people walking up and down';* and meant every word she said.

• • •

Thousands of people, every week, partake in an experience that cannot fail to move them in some way, as they wait in St. Peter's Square, Rome, for the papal blessing. Catholic and non Catholic alike testify to a sense of expectation; a feeling of elation; the 'togetherness' of the crowd (there from all over the world), as they wait patiently and reverently to partake in a ceremony perhaps not necessarily understood, but certainly 'felt'.

Holding out an assortment of objects of all shapes and sizes for the blessing, believer and non-believer together, participate in a sacred ritual, a never to be forgotten moment. It is a moment when our spirit, our true self, has dominance; the material world, second place; the papal blessing perhaps a good example of human kind reaching out to the 'invisible', moving onto a higher plane of thought.

There is 'a rising tide of consciousness leading to a flood of understanding, an awakening', as Sir George Trevelyan, one of the great pioneers of New Renaissance thinking, tells us, 'a spiritual awakening in our time; an awakening from 'the sleep of the senses' in which we mistake our bodily identity for our 'ultimate essence'.

Many writers and philosophers of our day, both secular and non-secular, are taking up the theme of the potential catastrophic times we are living in, while at the same time agreeing that our troubles are slowly, but surely, bringing in a new age that will gradually move away from our materialistic, 'greedy', 'me', society.

It seems to be that there is evolving a worldwide move to a more thoughtful, inner consciousness where, according to Sir George Trevelyan, we have less influence over the collective, but a great deal of influence on our own individual response, and even more so on in the inner attitude we adapt towards life. 'We can,' as Sir George suggests, 'try out the power of living ideas.'[8]

A recently published book, *God is Back*, which is a collaboration by an atheist and a Catholic, aims to chart how the global rise of faith is changing the world,[9] while President Obama, in his book *The Audacity of Hope*, tells us of the remarkable ability of evangelical Christianity to thrive, 'growing by leaps and bounds', in modern, high-tech America. He gives a moving account of the various explanations for this success, including the need of thousands of Americans to know that there is something more to life than the daily round, the common task; 'they (Americans) are deciding that their work, their possessions, their diversions, their sheer busyness are not enough. They need an assurance that somebody out there cares about them, is listening to them – that they are not just destined to travel down a long highway toward nothingness.'[10]

• • •

David Muckle from Alnwick, Northumberland, joined the Fifth Royal Northumberland Fusiliers (the army) in 1941 and he served as a soldier at Dunkirk. He returned home before being posted to Singapore and he was at Singapore when it fell.

Captured by the Japanese, David was in prison in Burma and Thailand and was put to work on the Burma/Thailand railway. As with the other prisoners, he suffered a dreadful time – ill, emaciated, ulcerated legs... . His mother, back home in

Northumberland, eventually received word from the War Office saying he was missing. She refused to accept that he was dead, always believing that he would return, even though others insisted there was little hope.

So insistent was she that he was alive, that a friend suggested she should go to a special meeting to be held at a Spiritualist church, a place she had never been to before. Finally, and rather reluctantly, agreeing to go, David's mother found herself in a packed church and, amazing as it was, the medium picked her out from all the crowd to address. The medium described seeing a tall thin man (which he was). She said he had bad legs, malaria, and described him as being emaciated but that he was strong, and he would soon meet a great white lady who would stop and shake his hand. This happened not long after. The lady was Lady Mountbatten who was visiting the troops. Out of the huge crowd assembled to greet her, she picked David and two other soldiers and shook hands with them. David was hospitalised, then months later, in 1944, he eventually returned home.

• • •

Does the hunger for belonging, for believing, the unease, the restlessness, the 'fear' displayed throughout our world signal the time for a new direction, for the spiritual awakening talked about for so long? Is this perhaps leading into our time for reflection, for a re-thinking of our own personal attitude towards life, for finding our own 'moment of truth', time to find our own 'inner way'?

Probably the most natural and the simplest (apart from prayer which we will come to in a later chapter) of all the avenues we could explore on the road to finding our inner way, is first to take time to be quiet, find stillness; slowly, through the quiet, through the stillness, moving into reflection.

Reflection; to be thoughtful, when, apart from the pleasurable experience of, say, reliving happy memories, we might think long and hard about a particularly disturbing circumstance and on reflection, feel we have a few answers and know how to proceed. (Reflection is a natural state we must all have practised countless times in our lives.)

From reflection, we might slip into day dreaming, another usually pleasurable experience and from where some of our greatest art and scientific discoveries have been made.

Reflection, day-dreaming, silence, but it is the totality, the 'silence of the silence', that many people find difficult to engage in. Our world today, where we are bombarded by noise on all sides, is not conducive to silence. Newspapers, even fashion magazines are remarking on it. One well-known and authoritative magazine in particular that has a column devoted to 'trends', sites 'silence' as a 'going up' trend; 'silence'! A 'going up trend'!! Imagine that, coming from a state of the art, up to date, smart, 'with it' magazine; and to further quote, "silence', the new luxury in a twittered out world' (quiet carriages to be quiet), all applauded by the model Cindy Crawford who claims the luxury of 'time by herself'.

So conditioned are we to living surrounded by noise, living perhaps with a background sound such as music, ticking clocks, voices from inside the home, voices from outside the home, the sound of traffic. It is not only a difficult feat to find a quiet place to be solitary, but if we do find one, it may also be difficult, almost impossible, for us to tolerate silence – at first. (Interesting to note that, we have a generation of children who are anxious and unsettled, many of them not seeming able to talk to each other without having to shout to make themselves heard. Recently, a headmistress reported that a class of six-year-olds in her school held a sponsored silence to raise money for charity. The result was both successful and surprising, the children, this class of six-year-olds, asking if they could do it all again!)

It was August 1914, and Private James Brown of the 1st North Staffordshire Regiment arrived, along with his regiment to join the Great War in France. On the 27th September, his wife wrote to him telling him the sad news that Prince, his favourite Irish terrier was missing. James replied, 'I am sorry that you have not found Prince. You are not likely to. He is over here with me.'

The dog had travelled over 200 miles through the south of England, succeeded in crossing the Channel, and then somehow managed to cross another 60 miles of war-torn French countryside to the one set of trenches on the front line near Armentieres, to be with his master. [11]

• • •

Hearing a well known personality, a celebrity, who is obviously a 'full-on', materially minded, blindly ambitious and self-proclaimed egocentric, in a radio interview the other day, enthuse about the power of the human spirit was an eye-opener for me.

The interviewee was meaning physical prowess, the ability to rise above all obstacles, to keep going, determination, beating the odds (probably not realising, not even having given a thought to the fact that the physical – is influenced, motivated, by the spirit). Listening to the interview, I immediately felt how privileged we are, those of us who have become awake to the power of the spirit in its fullest sense; awake to the clear message that human kind possesses abilities of which we are normally unaware, but which are, in fact, our natural inheritance.

What more could we ask for in life than to know that, whatever our circumstance, state, intention, there is always – whatever name we may care to use, a 'presence' there with us, waiting the chance to make itself known? There to love, guide, befriend, encourage, and never to let us down...this magic, this 'miracle of life', to be reached through our ability to use all the attributes we have in our spiritual (we already know about our physical), make-up; in other words, the ability to 'tune-in'.

We are already 'tuned in' to our inner self, our 'higher consciousness', when we listen to our dreams. When we trust that 'hunch', that first strong feeling that comes through intuition; see coincidence as more than just coincidence; recognise the strength of the physical as being directed by the spirit, and remembering, above all, that to be a whole, complete person, the spiritual and the physical must be in harmony.

To achieve a stronger connection, however, a deeper understanding of this burgeoning spiritual side of our nature, we must, as has already been stressed, make time to be quiet, to be 'still', slowly and carefully moving into the depth of silence.

• • •

'What lies behind us and what lies before us are tiny matters compared to what lies within us.'[12]

After the time to be quiet, to be still, to reflect; looking for that place of calm, that silence – and it could take weeks or months – (for some a life-time to achieve this state of mind), we must go within, and within, and within, to recognise our inner strength.

Go within and within and within, to gain a sense of self-worth. Within and within and within, knowing our spirit to be our true self. Within and within and within to find powers of which we are normally unaware. Within and within and within to bring the real self forward into daily life. Within and within and within, ever raising our thoughts, our consciousness, to the highest and best, to the universal energy, the life force, 'God'.

• • •

During demolition of the old Palace Hotel at Southport in 1969, the contractors were alarmed when a four ton lift began to move up and down by itself, this was despite the fact that the entire power supply had been cut off weeks before. The Electricity Board were called in to investigate and reported that there wasn't an amp going into the place, but just as they were leaving the lobby, the lift doors slammed shut and it shot up to the second floor. To rule out hoaxers, they set the brake on the lift and removed the emergency winding handle, but the next evening the lift performed again, for the benefit of a BBC television team![13]

● ● ●

Dark matter of an unknown form makes up most of the matter of the universe. Science does not understand what this substance is. The speed of light, once thought unbreakable, has been 'exceeded' in several recent experiments.

Mind over matter 'cannot be explained' scientifically.

Astronomers are finding planets where there were not supposed to be any, finding new worlds around surprisingly small stars.

Small changes to DNA that were once considered harmless enough to be ignored are proving to be important in human diseases, evolution and biotechnology; understanding the subtle dynamics of how genes work and evolve may reveal further insights into causes and cures for disease.

Work has started on the construction of the world's first purpose-built commercial space port in New Mexico that, those behind the project say, will help provide a new chapter in space exploration.

A lecture on genetic technology, the use of genetic engineering, posed more questions than it answered, the stark one being 'is it right?'

Sperm sorting: to be able to choose the sex of a child even before it is conceived.

'Yanking' any disease-causing micro organism out of the blood with magnets.

Fish can feel pain.

The dictionary definition of the word 'science' is a branch of knowledge requiring systematic study and method, especially dealing with substances, life, and natural laws: *life, and natural laws*. Amid all the excitement, and furore, and possibilities of the stupendous new technology we are living with, there are, and have been for over thirty years, a small but steadily growing band of highly respected scientists whose discoveries prove what religion has always believed; that human beings are far more than the physical body they inhabit. While in the past, individuals who showed ability in clairvoyance, in premonitions, past life experiences, a gift for healing – usually dismissed as some sort of confidence trick or freak of nature, the work of these scientists suggested that this ability was neither abnormal nor rare, but present in every human being.

'Their work hinted at human abilities beyond what we'd ever dreamed possible. We were far more than we realised. Far from destroying God, science for the first time was proving His existence – by demonstrating that a higher, collective consciousness was out there. There need no longer be two truths, the truth of science and the truth of religion. There could be one unified vision of the world.[14]

It would seem to be that although regular science continues in its endless pursuit to discredit and view with scathing anything that cannot be pinpointed or classified in one way or another in a laboratory, the power of the so-called supernatural or the 'paranormal', although not always visible is no less powerful in the presence of its 'invisibility'!

• • •

It was towards the end of the Second World War at South Shields, in the north of England. South Shields had been heavily bombed during the war because of its position near the River Tyne, where there was a lot of heavy industry; ship building and repair yards; shipping. Edith, a nine-year-old girl, deeply engrossed in playing at building a house in the rubble of a bombsite, was suddenly surprised to see a little girl of about five standing quietly staring at her, a few yards away. She had previously seen the little girl, a few times, but this time was different. Different, because she was wearing a beautiful, obviously new, party dress as she stood there silent, amid all the dirt and rubble, completely still, arms by her sides.

The little girl had black hair which stood out in contrast to the delicately coloured short pink dress with puffy sleeves; on her feet she wore the short white ankle socks and black shoes with a strap that were the fashion for most young girls at that time.

Edith asked her if she would like to play, and remembers telling her that she would have to go home first and get changed...and...then...she...disappeared...

Returning home from school the next day, Edith noticed a house with the curtains closed (a custom then when there was a death in the family). Two women were standing beside the window of the house, one having just come from inside informing the other that he had been in to see the little girl who had died there, and describing how she was 'laid out' in the pink party dress her mother had bought her for her birthday. Edith fell into a state of complete shock as she overheard the conversation.

• • •

Science has, for many years, been working towards developing new 'war games' for use in subversive activities, one in particular, various forms of 'mind control'. Much, it seems, has been accomplished, and many things that were thought to be impossible

47

to achieve have 'come to pass' thanks to MRS (a highly developed scanner). It seems that you can have a crude idea of what is going on in the mind, through the scanner, but if you micro-manage things too much you make a robot. (Micro-waves controlling a one syllable number in your head is supposed to be as far as experiments can go) and, on information relayed by one scientist, we know that science still cannot put a 'thought' into the brain.

According to an intelligence agency, it is not possible to do mind control yet, (mind control for reality), but, as was reported, 'someone, somewhere, will be working on it, we can be sure of that'.

• • •

The wonderful gift of 'memory' is still, apparently – this from a well-established neurologist – something that science cannot fathom, and recently, it was reported that a group of scientists marvelled at the way a blind man managed to manoeuvre his way around obstacles. It is common knowledge that police, all over the world, call in psychics from time to time to help in particularly difficult cases. (Years ago, the police in London regularly used the services of a medium with excellent results.) All this proves the point that the 'something else' factor is as prevalent in our 'ultra' modern world today, as ever it was; this in spite of the most recent and almost unbelievable advances made in both science and technology.

The something else factor; there is always a 'something else' that comes into the equation. To a scientist, it could be an accident of one sort or another in the laboratory leading him on to yet another clue in a discovery, another hint of a solution to a test; perhaps a sudden remembering of a previous problem, and the answer it had thrown up. Thomas Edison used to keep a pencil and paper on his bed-stand and he would write down ideas that came to him while he was sleeping. Physicist Niels Bohr visualized atomic structure when dreaming about the sun and planets. Nobel Prize winner Otto Loewi discovered mediation of nerve pulses in a dream.

'We leap,' in the words of psychologist Donald Norman, 'to correct answers before there are sufficient data, we intuit, we grasp, we jump to conclusions despite the lack of convincing evidence. That we are right more often than wrong, is a miracle.'[15]

Could it be that when we are right more often than wrong, it is because we are 'tuned in' to wavelengths of truth and harmony, our spirit able to access the infinite wisdom of the universal energy, the life force, God?

With an artist, a writer, a musician, the 'something else' factor could be inspiration; Mozart, in a letter to a friend, described his creative gift as one coming from 'outside himself'. Samuel Taylor Coleridge awoke with what he called 'a distant recollection' of the whole of 'Kubla Khan', which he wrote down without conscious effort, pausing only when interrupted by a visitor. By the time he returned to his room, the end of the poem was lost forever; gone, the flow broken, the work incomplete.

· · ·

With every day of every life come promptings, reminders, evidences of the spirit within that makes us who we *really* are. Coincidences to give us messages, show us the way; unexpected meetings that can change our whole pathway in life; opportunities that seemingly come from nowhere; dreams to influence, to teach, often giving us an understanding of another realm, another reality, where the impossible can happen and often does! Memory, to enrich and give comfort through the magical process that it is; inspiration, to help us create something special – but to do this we also need to be 'lit' from within – thought wherewith we can travel the Universe; be king for a day; send out love to anyone, anywhere; for thoughts are living things. (Is it not wonderful how people, lacking in a certain gift, maybe through a disability, often have a superabundance of another gift?)

• • •

Are we aware of the one true source we can turn to for guidance, help, inspiration, as we travel this often, stony, road...?

Are we becoming aware of our own true potential in life?

Are we aware of the potential we have to achieve great things?

As the 'ancients', the philosophers, the wise men, the teachers, have preached to us over centuries, everything is possible, and all is within. All is within.

• • •

Margaret has two young children and a very full life working as a nurse in a busy medical practice. She had never had any sort of strange experience before and not even thought much about such things until, one night, she swears she had a vision.

She was under great stress and worry at the time. She and her husband had, after a lot of thought, upgraded the family into a much bigger and more expensive property that they knew they could 'just about' afford, if all continued to go well.

Margaret then started to worry about it. With sleepless nights, fraught with doubt and anxiety, she made herself ill thinking about it. She had confided in her grandmother, whom she was especially close to, before they made the decision to move, and her grandmother had advised her to go ahead, but the worry continued.

Then, again, before any final decision was made, she had a dream. More than a dream, she insists. Her guardian angel appeared to her, and although she had not thought like this before, she just knew it was her guardian angel; with no wings, but appearing all in white.

The angel asked her what she could do to help, then said that all would be well, to go ahead with the move, it would be the right thing to do, but she would suffer a loss.

Two months later, her grandmother, who had not been ill, passed away.

Margaret says of course she was 'devastated' by this, but did still feel comfort and peace because of the presence she had experienced in her vision; feeling the same comfort and peace after her grandmother's passing as she had on the morning after (the dream/vision.)

• • •

Right across the ages and from all circumstances in life, men and women have found God. They have found the 'something else' that leads them on to aim for the highest and best in what life can offer; the highest and best that is out there, beckoning, waiting for each, for every one of us. They have found their rainbow; they have found their pot of gold at the end of their rainbow, realising priceless treasures of a spiritual nature to be the pinnacle of a life; indestructible, tangible, all embracing, and eternal.

They have learned to listen to that inner voice of spirit, to be 'in tune' with their spiritual self, to connect, knowing themselves to be much greater than this small physical space we inhabit on the earth plane.

They understand this life to be no more than a school where we learn life's lessons before moving on to the 'greater reality', the spirit world. They have tried to be good and kind and caring – of all life, respecting all life, respecting 'Mother Earth'.

They have learned, in all this, the secret of being true to one's self, of acting with character, courage and dignity. Always striving to live in love, truth, and harmony, they have learned that when we 'fall down', as we all do from time to time, there is always the 'something else' waiting to pick us up, point us in the right direction, show us the way, get us back on track.

• • •

Life goes on, changes come and go; additions and subtractions, paths re-routed, bridges burned, bridges crossed; nothing stays the same. Additions and subtractions; bringing with them a certain amount of happiness, a certain amount of pain, but this *is* life, this ever-changing pattern, this is life's journey; nothing stays the same.

During a period of change, there are usually 'bumps' along the way. Moving into a new sphere of life often takes, along with the rewards – 'is it a little love that grows and blossoms into something deeper every day', the casualties – 'maybe a little hurt that, left untended, changes things and turns some friend away'. Addition and subtraction, the pattern changes every day and in the present climate of our world, the time, as you might say, is 'ripe' for change. Ripe for change to a more spiritual society, where we care for each other, where we care about each other and, as has already been said in an earlier chapter, where we move on from a greedy 'me' phase.

Magazine articles, political commentaries, radio talks, appear to press on with questions and commentaries about our moral status, and yet another headline in a newspaper – this one in *The Sunday Times* – referring to the state of certain financial affairs, reports, 'Finance minister attacks bankers' greed and finds God'.[16] Attacking the 'troubling absence of clear moral purpose' in banking, Lord Myners, the minister appointed to clean up the City, told *The Sunday Times* that he was worried he may have 'neglected' the moral purpose of life, continuing to state that: 'This is very evident in the financial community – that money has become everything. People have lost their sense of purpose. The absence of clear moral purpose is something that is very troubling,' he said.

In this worrying, and for many, catastrophic time in which we live, there is still, and always will be, hope. Faced with troubles on so many fronts, climate change, financial irregularities, a war-torn world with terrorists trying to get the upper hand, the other side of life is ever on guard, patiently watching and waiting, knowing the chance to step in will come, and we can see it happening now, as I write these words. This, our 'now' time, is rapidly becoming a time of great hope for moral and civil renewal. A time for politics of the common good, a time for remembering what it means to be a citizen, a time to reflect on moral and spiritual questions, and our time to fulfil the old prophesy, that this would be the age of a spiritual revolution.

How is your own, personal journey progressing? Have you experienced perhaps a dream, a coincidence (even a small one), maybe a relevant conversation you could note down at the back of the book? Has something happened to make you stop and think, 'Well...'?

As we begin to realise, if we haven't already done so, that there *is* more to life than the daily round, the common task, work, possessions, diversions, sheer busyness; that somebody out there does care about us, that somebody out there does listen to us, and that we are not just destined to travel down a long highway toward nothingness...

...Let's walk a good walk!

Chapter Three

Strange, unexpected things that happen in life all the time

'If we do not expect the unexpected, we will never find it'.[1]

THAT STRANGE, WEIRD, AND wonderful things do happen in life, and are happening all the time, is true; and that they often happen with no evident explanation, no apparent reason, is also true; not apparent at the time perhaps, but it is said, that everything happens for a purpose.

Alberobello is a quiet little place, a small town in the region of Puglia, sunny Southern Italy, and it was here that Padre Pietro, and other witnesses, experienced two amazing phenomena. Padre Pietro, fifty-nine years old, a parish priest since 1990, is the founder of a small congregation called 'The Missionaries of Our Lady of the Quarry'. He lives in a modest house in Alberobello, and it is in his own words that we hear the story of the two Icons.

'It was on the 3rd of May 2003, around six in the evening. I had gone to my room to take some medication when I noticed that the Icon, which represents the Madonna with Child, hanging above my prayer kneeler, had spots on its face. Because I have poor eyesight I touched the Image and felt that it was wet. I called my fellow members (confreres) and all of us could see that she was shedding tears.'

She was, in fact, weeping blood. The phenomenon lasted thirty minutes and was recorded on video tape. Padre Pietro wiped the blood with a handkerchief and sent it to a laboratory to be tested.

One year later, on the 27th May 2004, the 'phenomenon' was repeated on another Icon, also belonging to Padre Pietro. This time it was the face of Jesus as it appears on the Shroud of Turin, and this time it was more than a weeping Icon, according to the words of author Renzo Allegri, it was a bloody sweat. 'The face of Jesus was striped by seven streaks of blood that trickled down from the forehead, along the cheeks, over the beard, and running over the picture frame of the Icon.'

Padre Pietro, frightened, called out to all who were in the house to come and see; he then telephoned the police, the parish priest and the doctor. This phenomenon lasted for one and a half hours and was witnessed by about fifty people.

Once more Padre Pietro collected some of the blood and sent the sample to the same laboratory where he had sent the blood that had appeared on the Face of the Virgin Mary. This laboratory, the Genetics Forensic Laboratory of the University of Bologna is one of the most prestigious in Europe, fitted out with the most modern equipment and a team of researchers, doctors and biologists, University Professors. The laboratory, apparently, specialises in everything related to DNA; it works with Secret Services and police from many countries and is in contact with other similar laboratories in other countries.

After carrying out all the tests, the laboratory researchers sent Padre Pietro an official document relating to both the tears (blood) of Mary and the blood of Jesus.

The document states;

'The blood is human blood; group AB male and was found to be identical in the two samples tested: the blood from the tears of the Icon of the Virgin and the blood that appeared on the face of Jesus, are the same. The configuration of the genetic features found in the Y chromosome does not correspond to any of the configurations present in the worldwide data bank where the data of 22,000 male subjects from 187 different populations is stored.

The blood is so rare that it 'must be considered' as almost unique. By calculation, the statistical probability of finding, in the course of millennia, a typology of the same blood type, is almost nil: the mathematical probability of this happening is in the order of one in 200,000,000,000: (200 billion): that is: 30 times larger than is the population of the whole Earth today.'[2]

What the scientists are saying is that this blood could only belong to one person and to one person only in all of humanity's history. Therefore, it comes from a man who had no ancestor and had no descendant. One researcher wrote to Padre Pietro: "Faced with the results of the analysis, I could not succeed in hiding my tears." Another wrote to him, "This is real human blood but it seems to really come from another world."

• • •

Mark Bredin, musician, was travelling in a taxi late one night through London after a concert, when suddenly, he felt certain that, at the next traffic lights – Queensway – a taxi would jump the lights and hit them, side-on. But it seemed ridiculous to tap the driver on the shoulder and say 'Excuse me but…' so he said nothing.

At the next traffic lights, a taxi ignored a red light and hit them side-ways on.

• • •

'This is real human blood but it seems to really come from another world'. Strange, weird, and wonderful things that happen in life. Jean, travelling in a local bus, sent a text message to her brother in Australia and had a reply before she even had time to put her phone away in her handbag; an American magazine, *Entertainment Weekly*, published (limited edition) on 20th August 2009, shows moving pictures when opened. A slim magazine, with a wafer thin screen and mini-speaker, it allows readers to watch a video, while a new mobile phone obeys voice instructions to find telephone numbers and music tracks...

Is it not maybe even easier now, because of all the marvels portrayed by science and technology, and our better understanding and familiarity with terms such as 'e-mailing', 'websites', 'wavelength frequency', 'laser beams', 'cyber space', to accept the truth of another world, of other worlds! (The first official government site in the world to document UFO sightings collapsed under a stampede by the public to gain access – the website was 'overloaded' and 'crashed'.) How far-fetched is it to think like that; to believe in a spirit world that is really our 'home'; 'from whence we came'. "We all know our lives on earth are incomplete", words from a Catholic Priest. How much literature, and art, and music, and how many hymns have been devoted to the theme. A popular song performed at funerals is 'Going Home'.

One of the researchers to the authenticity of the blood on the Icons remarked that both Mary and Jesus must have had unique bodies and they wanted us to know. The ecclesiastical authorities are aware of all the facts and are investigating and evaluating them but, as Renzo Allegri comments, the scientific results lead us to think that we may have here, a supernatural sign of exceptional importance.

Strange occurrences, seemingly impossible situations, signs, clues abounding in every life, if we would only think them through; take time to 'read' them, understand them, while at the same time trying to accept that 'yes', perhaps everything does happen for a reason, that there *is* a purpose in everything.

We are all on our own road, making our own way in life. Sometimes we seem to be at a standstill, sometimes forging ahead, but we must never forget that we don't travel alone. And in the bleak days, this is when we especially need the 'faith' – but is it not *more* than 'faith' – that comes to us; sometimes in a big 'shout', sometimes so subtle that we might even ignore it, but it is there, *it is there*, and ours for the taking if we would only give it recognition. When we are ready to take a new step in life, follow a new direction, the way 'will be shown'; and when we are ready to accept yet more knowledge, understanding even more the ways of the spirit, it too will be shown. When the pupil is ready, the teacher will appear.

Film star Shirley MacLean was in her local library when the book, *The Sleeping Prophet*[3] fell out of its place on the shelf and landed at her feet. She picked it up and decided to read it. It changed her life. Have you thought very deeply about the strange things that have happened in your own life, maybe to help you to see 'sense' in something, maybe to give you a nudge in a decision, a sharp shock to galvanize you into necessary action at some point...(reading the tea-leaves is not the only way to connect!!!)

• • •

Ivan, an artist, would not call himself religious, but he does believe that he has an 'angel' who looks after him. One year, it was the start of the school summer holiday, he had a family to look after, he was hard up and had no chance of even part-time teaching, nothing. Things looked hopeless.

Amazingly to Ivan, a former colleague came to the door. She did promotion work for companies. The artist doing the designs

– illustrations for gas cookers, a letter box etc. – had let them down. Ivan gladly accepted the work, one design a day drawing and painting, for six weeks. As he said, it was a 'God send'.

Another time when he was desperate for money, it was Christmas Eve. Again, amazingly, a friend knocked on the door and bought one of his pictures for £400.

Ivan says that those sort of things happen to him all the time, making him accept that, however bad it gets, something always turns up.

• • •

Ancient civilisations left many signs suggesting that they had knowledge and understanding reaching far into our own era and possibly beyond. Cave drawings and other carvings with figures, some of which were even robed (early people were usually naked?), sometimes in garments that could be taken for space suits; figures that could be taken for astronauts, our space men with gloves, suits, headgear. People have talked for centuries about the possibility of visitors from other planets.

This year of 2009, and in particular the month of August, has seen more talk and celebration of man's first landing on the moon since the spectacular achievement itself, which happened in August, 1969. Of almost equal interest, is the effect the landing had on the lives of the twelve astronauts who made it, the ones who actually walked on the moon's surface. (Just by way of a coincidence, the death of Pete Conrad, the Commander of Apollo 12 Mission, and the third man to land on the moon, was due to a motorbike accident that happened at a place near his home in California, called Ojai. Ojai is the native American word for 'Moon'.)

The unhappy lives of the astronauts since the moon landings has been well recorded, and perhaps the words of Gene Cernan, the last man on the moon, who admits to disappointment with everything that has followed his experience with Apollo 17 says it all; 'It's tough to find an encore.' But surely, the reactions of the astronauts after such an unbelievable and sensational achievement – *and* experience – should have been predicted, if only through consideration of the question that must, in retrospect, have preyed on all their minds; 'Where do you go after you've been to the Moon?'

Charlie Duke, the tenth of the twelve human beings to land on the moon couldn't settle when he returned. He seriously disrupted life for his wife and children before finally coming to peace through faith in God. He now runs a ministry with his wife in Texas. The astronauts described the spectacle of seeing the earth from the moon in a similar way. Duke described the striking luminescence of our world, moving through the lonely black void of space; 'The planet was like a jewel, so colourful and bright that you felt you could reach up and grab it, hold it in your hands and marvel at it like the precious thing it is.'

Jim Irwin, the eighth man to land on the moon, was said to have heard God whispering to him at the foot of the Apennine Mountains on his return, and left NASA (the National Aeronautics Space Administration), for the church.

It was on the homeward journey that Apollo 14 astronaut, Ed Mitchell, the sixth man to land on the moon and who, with his commander Alan Shepard, carried out the first lunar landing scientific investigations, had not so much a normal religious experience, but a 'blinding epiphany of meaning', sometimes called by Eastern religions an 'ecstasy of unity'. It happened in an instant, while he was staring out of the window in the Kittyhawk when he experienced this, the strangest feeling that he would ever have; a feeling of *connectedness*; as if all the planets and all the people of all time were attached by some invisible thread. Overcome by this sense of 'oneness', this dramatic revelation, he continued with his navigation while feeling distanced from his body, as though someone else was going through the motions.[4]

• • •

Susan Finden was well used to Casper disappearing; she took him from a rescue home some years ago and named him after the cartoon ghost Casper, 'as he has always been a free spirit and had a habit of walking off'. She once had to walk a mile-and-a-half with a cat basket to bring him back from a car park; but this time was different.

Casper had been disappearing at the same time each day for almost a year, and she had no idea what he got up to, that is, until someone from the local bus company at his home in Plymouth, Devon, contacted her and told her the story.

At 4.00 each day, Casper joins the queue of people waiting to board the number 3 bus into the centre. He sits quietly in the queue, then trots on board and curls up on a seat for the ride, never causing any trouble. He stays on board as the bus empties, then turns, ready for the return trip. He is a well-known commuter on the bus service and amuses passengers during their journey, according to a spokesman for the company. He is now so well known the bus drivers are aware at which stop to let him off, when he wants to go home. (He usually jumps up and lets *them* know anyway.) A notice has been put up in the bus drivers' rest room in Plymouth asking them to look after Casper, the black and white cat, if they spot him sneaking on board.

• • •

Edgar Mitchell, writing about the homeward journey from the moon, told of a 'sense of unreality here, with the absence of gravity and the tapestry of blackness broken only by an overwhelming glitter of stars that surround our craft'; and, as experienced by the others, 'the intricate beauty of Earth overwhelmed the senses'. He felt a real physical yearning, a 'strange nostalgia' for the world he'd just left and knew he would never see again, at close quarters, but it was to be the overpowering sense of *connectedness*, his 'blinding epiphany of meaning', that would change the course of his life soon after the return to earth. He glimpsed an 'intelligence' in the Universe, and felt connected to it. He was fascinated with this feeling of *transcendence* and later, he left NASA and founded the Institute of Noetic Sciences (having to do with the mind, or intellect), his aim being to reconcile Science with Religion, in that great mystery, consciousness itself.

Serious studies and research into paranormal phenomena began, such as the health benefits of healing, acupuncture, meditation, and extrasensory perception (ESP).[5]

His path in life now set, as if in stone.

• • •

Shortly after my writing about the moon landings, and with no 'follow up' to their great adventure, leaving some of the astronauts 'disappointed', to say the least, an announcement was made yesterday, 24th September 2009 to the world, stating that water has been found on the moon. With mounting excitement as to this discovery, scientists are now talking about the possibility – in the far distant future – of earthlings moving to the moon!; – setting up space stations with a view to the exploration of further planets, and the eventuality of leaving earth, and making our home in far away, deep space.

(Is the, to *some* anyway, improbability of the spirit world as our 'true' home becoming less and less?)

Many 'Out of Body Experiences' (OBEs), reported by ordinary, on the earth plane, mortals, describe the same sort of feelings as told by the astronauts. They tell of feeling at one with nature, the rocks, the sky, the sea. Sometimes of everything being surrounded by a golden glow of light, or a bright light, all this accompanied by a most wonderful feeling of peace, security, happiness; and it seems that this experience often changes lives into being more caring, thoughtful, loving, not only towards other people but towards the Animal Kingdom, towards the whole of nature its-self.

Mavis tells us; "Years ago my husband and I and our children were visiting a National Park and stopped to have a picnic lunch beside a stream. Afterwards the children were playing, and my husband busy with the car, and I found myself alone and started climbing around on some rocks out into the centre of the stream. I sat down on one of the rocks and became fascinated with the ripples on the surface of the water and the way they were sparkling in the sun. Then, it was as though time stood still. I don't know how long I sat there and stared at what now looked like thousands of sparkling lights. I lost all consciousness of anything else in my surroundings. Later, as I drifted back into my usual consciousness, I was thinking that our whole world is a reflection of many aspects of some great oneness that includes everything that is.

"Sometimes when I am at the beach, looking out over the ocean, I think about the other side, far across the ocean. One day my thoughts took a different direction and I became conscious of a more distant shore, much more distant than anything on Earth, over some vast expanse of space. It seemed very personal to me, as if I had some close connection with it, like it was another home, with people I loved and from whom I was now separated. I think of this every once in a while and wonder if I will ever get back there."[6]

• • •

Joan's OBE; "Neither my father nor my mother went to church nor had any religious belief. I have not been christened and was always encouraged from an early age to sort out my own feelings about religion. Any religious education I had at school I barely tolerated. I had left art college, but it was about two years before that when I was out walking with my sister while on a holiday in Cornwall. We were walking along the beach, my sister had walked on in front of me; I was left alone. It was as if time had stood still. I could think of nothing, I only felt I was 'somewhere else'. I was part of something bigger and absolutely beyond me. My problems and my life didn't matter at all because I was such a tiny part of a great whole. I felt a tremendous relief. I was aware of my eyes not looking at, but feeling, the beauty of everything that was there for eternity. I have never forgotten that day. Because of that experience I have become extremely interested in many different types of religions and philosophies, and have found many descriptions similar to mine." [7]

• • •

Out-of-body experiences can take on a physical form, such as the one that happened to Anne one day when she was swimming.

'I was seventeen years old and my brother and I were working at an amusement park. One afternoon quite a few of us decided to go swimming. Someone said, 'Let's swim across the lake.' I had done that often enough but that day, for some reason, I went down, almost in the middle of the lake…I kept bobbing up and down, and all of a sudden, it felt as though I were away from my body, away from everybody, in space by myself. Although I was stable, staying at the same level, I saw my body in the water about three or four feet away, bobbing up and down. I viewed my body from the back and slightly to the right side. I still felt as though I had an entire body form, even while I was outside my body. I had an airy feeling that's almost indescribable. I felt like a feather.'

• • •

Jane was driving home alone one evening across Exmoor and there was the most beautiful moon, which made her think about her mother – who would have loved the sight. Thinking deeply about her mother, she also recalled that her mother's favourite song was 'O Silver Moon'.

Just then, the announcer on the radio said, 'And now we will play you "O Silver Moon" ', which they did.

. . .

Strange, unbelievable things that happen in life all the time, pulsing the moment of our being, giving it a special significance, a breath of life all its own.

. . .

In the summer of 1995 a group of friends travelling around Egypt and Israel decided to do a night climb, up Mount Sinai. A tiring climb, but as they said later, well worth it, the views of the sunrise were spectacular. Two of the group wandered off to take photographs and lost the rest of the party, who thought they were ahead, and so began their own descent.

After wandering lost for some time on a treacherous path, huge boulders precariously placed, ledges and other hazards – it turned out that they were on the wrong path. They began to pray, not knowing what else to do, and becoming increasingly alarmed, one of the two cried out aloud hysterically for help. Then a person dressed in a long white robe appeared to them, a little way off. They followed him but just as they seemed to catch up with him, he would disappear then turn up again out of nowhere. Always keeping his distance ahead, they followed him until they reached the safety of other travellers.

In a similar story that also happened some years ago, a family, mother and father, Dorothy and Jim, along with their teenage daughter Susan, were travelling in a mobile home through old

Yugoslavia to reach Greece, just as the troubles were starting. What should have been an exciting trip, proved to be one of fear and danger, and as they later said, it was their faith and their prayers (they are strong Catholics) that kept them going. There were road-blocks, they were 'threatened' by 'gangs', who tried to intimidate them, once even shaking their mobile home violently, but they managed to escape. Too late to turn back, they just had to plough forward, not knowing what was going to be around the next corner.

Their final terrifying experience occurred when a huge crowd, gathered together at one side of their mobile home, preventing them from moving, had to be 'faced'. Jim stood on the step and remonstrated with them, trying to explain that they were just innocent travellers…and then, one man, although he was standing at the back, stood out from the crowd. In some strange way, he seemed to be completely visible, in his white robe, and with a face like Jesus. He was signalling to them, and they seemed to understand what he was trying to say. He was telling them to move 'quickly', not to delay, to 'go, go!', even pointing the way to them. Somehow or other they did exactly what he had tried to tell them to do, and finally, and thanking God for his blessed intervention, they reached the safety of Greece, then home.

It would appear that the travellers in the two accounts just given actually 'saw' their helpers, their guides, angels, or whoever their help had come from, but in the next few experiences, recounted in his book *The Third Man Factor, True Stories of Survival in Extreme Environments*, author John Geiger writes about 'unseen but benevolent presences'. He tells of Frank Smythe's experience during the gruelling 1933 British Everest Expedition when, the last man to press forward to the top, Frank was aware of an 'invisible' companion who both comforted and reassured him, after his companions had been forced to retreat, and he was now in the so-called 'death zone'. Weak and disillusioned, the comforting presence became stronger as he made his way back to base camp, where he was finally 'persuaded', by the expedition leader, to write the experience into the official record. He wrote: 'All the time that I was climbing alone, I had a strong feeling that I was accompanied by a second person. The feeling was so strong it completely eliminated all loneliness I might otherwise have felt. It even seemed I was tied to my "companion" by a rope, and if I slipped "he" would hold me. I remember constantly glancing back over my shoulder.'

• • •

The clock on All Saints Church in Sudbury, Suffolk, began to strike thirteen at the end of January, 2009. Neither the vicar nor clock engineers could explain why the 130-year-old clock was striking the extra hour, believed to be a bad omen. The vicar said that the clock also struck thirteen shortly after he joined the parish four years ago.

• • •

Ron DiFrancesco, working at his desk on the eighty-fourth floor of the South Tower of the World Trade Centre, New York, on the day of the terrorist attack, 11th September, 2001, *knows* that he was 'led' to safety by a 'presence'. Surviving the devastating impact, when he was 'hurled' against a wall and showered with debris, he made his way to a stairwell (the trading floor he had just left no longer existed). With intensifying smoke, gasping for air, people in panic, including DiFrancesco, trying to get this way and that way, he heard a voice. It addressed him by name. The voice was insistent, but encouraging, and accompanied by a vivid sense of a physical presence. 'Somebody lifted me up. I was "led" to the stairs. I don't think somebody grabbed my hand, but I was definitely led.'

Finally, after more 'scares', the 'presence' led him to safety. He was the last person out of the South Tower. [8]

• • •

Just at a time when an increasing number of people are showing interest in anything to do with the so-called 'paranormal', we have a 'fairly new' form of – is it – 'spirit communication? Orbs! Orbs have started to appear regularly on photographs since the use of digital cameras and now thousands (they are usually round but it appears they can be all shapes and sizes and colours) are materialising every day. Orbs, being a relatively new 'phenomenon', have not as yet been wholeheartedly accepted as coming from another realm. Much more investigation into their substance and origin has yet to be 'carried out' before they can be taken seriously. There are sceptics as to the truth that orbs are from another realm or are simply 'dust' or other minute debris floating in the air. One knowledgeable critic says he has never seen a photograph with an 'orb' that has been taken *without* a flash. Television presenter Noel Edwards believes in certain paranormal phenomena including orbs; he explained his theory to a *Mirror* reporter. 'Orbs' are little bundles of positive energy; they come in all shapes and sizes. We are all made up of energy – we vibrate all the time.'

(Everything is vibrating energy, and each of us has a personal vibration – a frequency of energy held moment by moment in our spirit, thoughts, emotions, and body – that communicates who we are to the world and helps shape our reality.)

'It is inconceivable to me [Noel Edmonds] that when we die, that energy just disappears.' It is interesting to hear all the talk there is, especially of late, about our being 'made up' of energy. This understanding seems to have taken hold in so many minds; even six-year-olds now use the word in a prayer at school: 'Dear God, thank you for giving me the energy to go to school and

68

do my work.' Eric Clapton, on an *Arena* television programme talked to Melvin Bragg about 'energy'. saying, 'We're all going to be moving around in some other area – that all this energy just doesn't stop.'

• • •

Jane O'Neill, severely affected by a serious accident she witnessed on her way to London airport when she helped to free badly injured people from a wrecked coach, suffered weeks off work and strange, waking visions, some of which were accurate.

One day in Fotheringhay Church, she was so impressed by a picture behind the altar that, later, she mentioned it to a friend who had been with her; but her friend said she hadn't seen any picture. So puzzled was Jane by this, that she rang the lady cleaner and asked her about it. The lady told her that there was no such picture.

The two friends revisited the church and to Jane's surprise, the inside was quite different to what she had seen before – it was much smaller – and the picture was not there.

She asked an expert on East Anglican churches, who put her in touch with a historian who knew the history of Fotheringhay. He told her that the church she had 'seen' had been the church as it was more than four centuries ago; it had been rebuilt in 1553.

• • •

Klaus Heinemann holds a PhD in experimental physics and worked for many years in materials science research at NASA, UCLA, and as a research professor at Stanford University. He has recently co-authored a book *The Orb Project*, in which he asserts that his working theory is that orbs are emanations from spirit beings. 'Orbs are a non-physical, real phenomenon that can be detected by physical means – but this field of research is in its infancy.' Professor Heinemann does say, however, that 'dust particles, pollen, or other moisture droplets in the air can produce images that may in some respects resemble true orb photographs', and that care must be taken to assess the evidence; he continues, 'Some camera mechanisms in certain circumstances will produce false pictures of orbs.' The professor has worked on healing the 'commonly perceived rift between science and spirituality' and lectures on expanding perception.

Thinking about 'expanding perception' reminds us that we none of us appreciate the extent of our own inner potential; so many energies around us, we only see and feel a tiny fragment of what is there; of the universe. Take the condition known as to be 'unconscious', meaning to be 'not conscious', not aware. It is a condition that is now disputed, with many people accepting the possibility that from the inner depths of the debilitated person can come a 'knowing', an 'awareness', often proved but not yet registered by medical science.

Annie Laird tells a remarkable story of such an experience, where she had undeniable proof that a dying man, supposedly 'unconscious', knew exactly what was happening only an hour or so before his death.

Annie and her mother sat one at each side of her uncle Wilf's bed as he lay dying. More out of this world than in it, it was distressing to see him so, especially for Annie's mother – he was her eldest brother – and they had always been close with a sibling 'love' that had grown stronger over the years. As Annie and her mother sat there, they were unable to help Wilf in any way except through 'prayer', which they both fervently believed in, and this they did. As they sat at either side of the bed, they each held one of his hands in their own two hands, Annie's mother, in a slow, mournful voice crying, 'He's so – cold – his hands are – so – cold,' as they sat there praying and sending love out to this special uncle and brother.

Years later, at a church service in a spiritualist church, the medium spoke to Annie, asking her if she remembered sitting by the bedside of a dying man. Annie had no recollection of such an incident and said so, but the medium insisted, saying, 'You were with another woman.' Still Annie felt vague about it until the medium continued with, 'You sat one at each side of the bed praying and sending out love to the man.' Then she remembered and listened in astonishment as the medium went on to say, 'You sat one at each side of the bed, holding his hands; the other lady said, "His hands are – so – cold, – so – cold" '...exactly in the slow, mournful way that her mother had spoken. Shaken by this evidence, Annie was thrilled to hear the medium continue, telling her that he had returned to say 'thank you' for all the love and prayers sent out to him that night; that they had helped his passing, and he was with them, returning their love.

Annie had, for many years, believed that there was no such thing as being totally 'unconscious'. That, somehow or other, there would be an 'awareness' to love, concern, 'prayer', and she was always careful not to say anything that wasn't 'positive' when beside someone who was seriously ill; while maybe others would remark that the 'ill' person couldn't hear or understand' anyway. Now, with this evidence, she had her proof.

• • •

Strange, weird, and wonderful things happen in life, all the time, often with no explanation, for no apparent reason (have *you* any such experience you could note down at the back of the book?) but it is said that everything happens for a purpose. There was the lady who heard the stars 'singing' as she made her way home late one night, deep in the heart of the country; she heard the music of the spheres. There were the campers sleeping near the site of an ancient castle, awakened by the tramp of feet, the thud of horses hooves, the clash of steel, murmurings, all sounds of a retreating or advancing army, as it played out perhaps some long-gone mediaeval battle. At Castle Rising, which is a twelfth-century site in Norfolk, 'paranormal investigators' were called in to conduct tests after sightings by visitors of figures dressed in monks' robes. 'The most common phenomenon seems to be people getting pushed about. They seem to be prodded and poked. We get these reports in about once a week.' Similar accounts come from Portland Castle in Dorset, and Scarborough Castle in Yorkshire. English Heritage staff have now been asked to log specific incidents reported by workers and visitors.

Ghostly stories involving cats, whose hair stands on end, and dogs, that growl or cower in a corner for no apparent reason, are many. Robert Morris, previously appointed to the Koestler Chair in Parapsychology at Edinburgh University, once took a whole menagerie with him to a supposedly haunted house in Kentucky to test their effectiveness as ghost detectors. In the party, there was a dog, a cat, a rat, and a rattlesnake. Each one of these creatures went into a room in which a murder had been committed, with their owner. The dog refused to go beyond the threshold. It snarled, and no amount of coaxing could stop it from struggling to get out. The cat leaped up onto its owner's shoulder and spent several minutes hissing and spitting at an empty chair in the corner of the room. The rat didn't show any emotion but the rattlesnake assumed an 'attack' position facing the same chair. None of the animals responded to any other room in the house.[9]

• • •

Research carried out by a Japanese scientist, shows that our hands, foreheads, and soles of feet emit light. Mitsuo Hiramtsu, a scientist at the Central Research Laboratory at Hamamatsu Photonics, has discovered that these three areas of the human body emit protons (a particle of matter with a positive electric charge). The light, said to be invisible to the naked eye, has been 'detected through the use of a powerful photon counter'.

It is well known and accepted that we all have an 'aura'; the energy field of the life force, the 'atmosphere' surrounding a person or thing, and now with this proof from Mitsuo Hiramtsu, it's official!

• • •

'It was a Friday. I had lectures from about 10.00 a.m. to 3.00 p.m. Three hall-mates had gone to London the day before. I didn't know when they were coming back. I attended the first two lectures and then at 12.00 I had a very strong desire to go back to Hall, and ran out of the university building. A bus turned up instantly (I was in quite a worried state actually) and I went back to Hall. Just as I entered the corridor, the telephone rang. Another bloke answered it and told me that my friends had been involved in a car crash the previous evening.'[10]

• • •

The 'aura', or ethereal light, has been compared to a 'white mist', but there are those who have developed the ability, in other words who are 'tuned in', to see the colours of the aura. These colours can indicate the state of health and well-being of a person, and can indicate character, but to read the aura is no mean feat as the colours can change from minute to minute.

Difficulties can come about as the colours change with different emotions and conditions; someone who becomes suddenly angry would flash 'red', while another person who is poorly would show 'brown'; white is for purity while gold means peace; green is for intellect and knowledge, pink is for love.

Displaying different colours in the aura can be likened to our reaction to 'sense', and 'feeling'; walking into a room and sensing a welcoming atmosphere; talking to someone and sensing a 'distant' feeling emanating from them. In those instances we are 'feeling', 'sensing', whereas the aura can be seen.

(Sir Arthur Conan Doyle, of Sherlock Holmes fame, was an untiring researcher into the paranormal, and reported the tale of a doctor he met while in Australia, who could walk behind a person in the street, and diagnose the disease they were suffering from.)

The aura can extend two or three feet, in all directions, from the body, and the bigger the aura, the more spiritual is supposed to be the person.

Author Ann Petri tells us of a little experiment we can try to 'feel' the aura.

'Place the palms of your hands together in front of you. Slowly, pull them apart until you feel a slight tingling. You will know the width of your aura as you repeat this exercise, very slowly. You can feel the energy build up between the palms of your hands. You can bounce the energy from one hand to another. (By simply joining the hands together and pulling them apart, the tension grows.)[11]

The dictionary definition of the word energy is, 'capacity for vigorous activity; ability of matter or radiation to do work'. Electricity is a form of energy, one that we don't want to meet up with, on a personal level...but physicist Brocklebank did, with extraordinary results.

Eric Brocklebank, sixty-four years old from Mansfield, found that he had an astonishing new ability after being struck by lightning on Sunday, 26th July, 2009. Eric had no knowledge of 'spirit', or spirit communication, but after this frightening experience, he could both 'see' and 'hear' spirit people.

It all started on the Sunday, as he drove an RAF cadet squadron (he is their chairman) to an airbase in Lincolnshire to take part in a marching competition. The cadets were ready to march when the heavens opened and heavy rain began to fall. He looked around and saw that lightning had struck the outer fence so he signalled to the cadets to take cover, finally getting them all on the bus and away to safety. 'Because they were wet through I went to the refreshment tent to get them hot drinks and something to eat. I was dishing out hot dog sausages into rolls, and serving cups of tea. Suddenly, as I was getting a sausage out of the pan, there was a big flash and a loud thump. That was it. The power and the pain were unbelievable. I turned round and said, "I think I've had an electric shock." '

Eric hit the ground, coming round every so often. 'When I was on the floor, it was really strange. It was as if I'd fallen asleep in a warm bath and was being pushed along. It felt endless and I kept waking up and opening my eyes. It seemed that the people around me were just images with no faces.'

The worried cadets tried to help Eric, but their sergeant told them not to touch him. In the ambulance, Eric stopped breathing. The ambulance crew revived him with small shocks. On arriving at the hospital, the staff thought he was 'dead' as the monitors were not responding due to the electrical charge in his body.

Consultants were arriving to see this 'novelty' case as it was rare to see someone survive such a massive electrical charge.

Waking up later in the hospital ward, Eric began to experience a series of strange events.

It was on the fourth or fifth day when, sitting up in bed, the ward was quiet, but 'I thought I must be going mad as I could hear people, but I couldn't see them. Then, "out of the blue", I saw a little girl at the end of my bed. At first, I thought I had imagined it. I blinked a few times but she was still there. She had black hair with a short fringe, and was wearing a pinafore dress. Her shoes had a little strap.' The little girl simply stood there, staring at him. Eric asked her what she wanted and in a soft voice, as though she was upset, she replied, 'I'm looking for my Nana. Where's my Nana?' Eric was talking to the little girl for some moments before the nurse arrived to give him his pills. He told her about the little girl but all she said was, 'We've got no little girl on this ward.'

Later, in the night, he suddenly saw an elderly gentleman walking up the ward in a charcoal suit. He stopped by Eric's bed and said, 'You've been struck by lightning, young man, haven't you? I was struck by lightning in 1957.' He continued, 'Don't worry about it. It's done me good. Whatever happens, just go and do it, go and do it.' Eric asked what he meant by that, but all he would reply was, 'You'll know when it happens. Just go and do it.'

The following morning, as breakfast was being served, a woman approached Eric and offered him a newspaper telling him that he was in the paper and must read it. 'I looked, and it wasn't me,' said Eric. 'It was the old gentleman I had seen. Then I thought I'd really "cracked".'

The strange 'phenomena' have stayed with Eric since his return home, and more amazing things seem to be happening to him all the time. He has sought advice from experts in this field, but it does seem that the ability to see and talk with spirit is the start of an unusual and dramatic pathway in life for Eric Brocklebank who insists, 'I'm a realistic person – things have to be in black and white for me…'.[12]

• • •

At the start of this chapter, we visited the little town of Alberobello, Southern Italy, and learned of strange, miraculous phenomena, the phenomena of the two Icons – 'Icons' that wept blood and that scientists proved was blood 'not of this world'.

Moving on, we thought about ancient civilisations and wondered if – through the evidence of various 'finds' – they *did* have the knowledge, the ability, to pre-empt our own times.

Thinking about the great adventure of the 'moon landings', it was no surprise to discover that the astronauts were 'changed' by their experience. The words of Ed Mitchell sum it up when he described, while staring out of the window on the homeward journey, 'the strangest feeling that he would ever have; a feeling of connectedness; as if all the planets and all the people of all time were attached by some invisible thread; a sense of oneness'. He felt distanced from his body, as though someone else was going through the motions.

And then we realised that people who have an OBE, 'out of body experience', report having a similar connectedness, feeling at one with nature, the sky, the rocks, the sea; a sense of 'oneness' with all living things. They also often report feeling 'distanced' from their bodies. Thinking about miraculous stories of survival, in impossible situations, where there is no hope, no help, that is, until the 'something else' intervenes, is always inspiring: the 'something else' that evidenced as a 'thought', an 'inner instruction', a silent voice; a 'physical presence', as it lifted Ron DiFrancesco up, then led him to safety, out of the blazing inferno that was the South Tower of the World Trade Centre, New York.

Having considered the fact that we are all of us, made up of energy, we questioned the assumption that 'Orbs' are little bundles of energy from the spirit world. Touching on 'ghost stories' and the 'aura' that surrounds each one of us (invisible to many naked eyes), the aura is now, incredible as it may seem, proven, through scientific investigation, to be, what seers and wise men have known through the ages, the 'energy field of the life force'.

• • •

It was a little after 2.00 on the morning of 27th January, 1957, when Martha Johnson saw herself travelling from Plains, Illinois, to visit her home 926 miles away in northern Minnesota. She saw her mother in the kitchen and, 'after I entered, I leaned up against the dish cupboard with folded arms. I looked at my mother who was bending over something white and doing something with her hands. She did not appear to see me at first, but she finally looked up. I had a pleased sort of feeling, and left.'

The following day, Martha's mother wrote to her daughter:

'It would have been about ten after two, your time. I was pressing a blouse here in the kitchen. I looked up and there you were at the cupboard just standing smiling at me. I started to speak to you and you were gone. I forgot for a moment where I was. I think the dogs saw you too. They got so excited.'[13]

• • •

The world is changing fast; so fast that even the engineers of it all can barely keep up. From one day to the next, we can't envisage what new bits of technology will emerge, with all the benefits they bring and all the problems. It is as if, while we were sleeping, changes to the very fabric of our lives, the social structure, shopping, travel, health, were 'magicked' into a new form of existence that 'just happened', and we were 'in it'; but basically, *people don't change.* Over centuries, we have moved through many eras of innovation and trauma, yet still, through it all, the human spirit prevails.

The spirit, ever strong and compelling, bidding us to bend with the changes and blend with the circumstances, nudges us to consider the 'illusion of the physical', the reality of spirit. Nevertheless, basically, people *don't* change. They still have the same needs, the same feelings – a same mysterious, hidden instinct. And although it is emerging that there is supposed to be a disinterest in church-going, and all that entails, it is not true to say that people have lost their inner desire to find a 'something' in life that gives meaning to it all.

A sect of Christians in the American Bible Belt, believe that 'the Supernatural is breaking into the world', and another sect believe that spirituality is coming through, in a secular society. Their church is not a building but a 'sacred space' where people are free to let go in any way – laughing, crying, hugging, emotion, intellect – all blending in an earth ritual; yet still there are many who believe that religion is at odds with an increasingly materialistic society. Old religions are being challenged, as never before, and according to one commentator, 'The old habitual church-going world has vanished very quickly.' Words to be disputed perhaps, when we see that still, in this modern, 'high tech' era, there continues to be a swathe of – 'core' believers, for whom their church, their own particular brand of 'religion', means everything. Many of us, who do think deeply about such things, are now perhaps not beholding to any one religion, but seeing the unity of the 'life force', the 'Universal Energy', as a benevolent presence.

(Now might be a good time for you to jot down at the back of the book any thoughts you have on the subject; your convictions, your own personal beliefs.)

With the churches, religion, becoming less influential in the present climate, there is a strong move to bring the secular world into the church. More and more churches are opening for lunch clubs, public 'social activities', craft fairs, coffee mornings, all helping people socially in difficult times. (Many soldiers in the Second World War fondly remember that it was only at the Salvation Army – always opposed to 'drink', where they could get a good old pint of beer.) With churches, of all religions, synagogues, opening doors and making the place available to the community, and this is now happening all over the country, is it partly trying to bring the community together, or – there is still the suspicion – is it the desire to bring people in for worship.

There is a thought that although 'Faith' has always played a part in life, now it is being 'driven out'. Most people would like a religious *home* not a religious prison; that they are spiritual but without the religious side; that religion, with all its trappings, has now to adapt to a new longing for something greater in us, that 'God' is just a word.

• • •

'The vision was so real it was uncanny. It happened months after my husband's death. In the vision, we were "locked" in a tight, loving, most comforting embrace and he had his face buried in my shoulder.

'Then I remember quite suddenly thinking, "How can this be?" How can he have his face pressed into my shoulder while wearing glasses? He had always had to wear glasses, from being a young lad. Slowly, he raised his head, and we stared lovingly into each other's eyes. To my complete amazement, he was not wearing glasses. On waking, I felt happy and "light", not how I would have expected to feel, having been in such close contact with the one person who was my "everything", and then to realise it was, after all, only a dream…

'But although, deep inside, I knew it was "more" than a dream, still "the glasses" worried me. I thought and thought about it all and discussed it with close friends, until, gradually, the answer dawned on me, and with the answer came proof of his continued existence and care for me. Of course! He didn't need glasses in the spirit world!

'No one needs any artificial aids; we are complete and in our prime!

'The experience has never left me.'

• • •

Life, in all its complexity, is no respecter of youth nor age, rich or poor. Life encourages us to appreciate the miracles that are with us, surrounding us, every day; the miracle of birth, of sight, of all the physical attributes; the miracle of thought, the miracle of true friends, of love; the 'wonders' of our world.

Alan Bean, the astronaut who became an artist on returning from his moon landing paints picture after picture of the experience, but talks movingly of his joy and appreciation on returning to earth's surface.

"The whole earth is the garden of Eden. We've been given paradise to live in. I think about that every day. We have never seen anything as beautiful as what we see when we walk out of the front door. That's why, when I came back from the spaceflight, I was a different person."[14]

Life also gives us the opportunity to recognise our spiritual self as the 'true self'. (Have you ever had a feeling, 'the awareness', that you are *more* than your physical body?) The more we try to link in, through thought and prayer, the more sensitive we become and the more aware of the spirit within.

Life gives us the opportunity to fine tune this body of ours, to be receptive to our 'inner self', which is the true self; the real you, the real me; realising that the physical is a body we need in order to live on the earth plane; sometimes described as an 'overcoat' we shed on passing.

Life, in all its complexity, presents us with the 'unexpected' that we sometimes find difficult to believe. The seemingly 'false', that turns out to be true. The 'bizarre', when reality can seem like a dream...'To live is but to dream; dreaming is living.'

Life; you and me; spirit in a physical body, careering through a succession of incidents and events that 'test', 'uplift', take us down...but always...always, there is the 'something'; watching; ever watching, and waiting, to reach out to us in hope, in love, in the unexpected, and in the certainty that, whatever else, we don't walk alone.

Chapter Four

Our spiritual inheritance

> The stars come nightly to the sky,
> The tidal wave unto the sea;
> Nor time, nor space, nor deep, nor high,
> Can keep my own away from me.[1]

NOR TIME, NOR SPACE, nor deep, nor high, can keep my own away from me. *'Can keep my own away from me'*; can we interpret those words to mean the family we are born into, the path we follow in life, the friends we make, the love we find as we travel along? –

> Asleep, awake, by night or day,
> The friends I seek are seeking me,
> No wind can drive my bark astray,
> Nor change the tide of destiny.

Can we see the words 'no wind can drive my bark astray, nor change the tide of destiny', as referring to our 'spiritual inheritance?' The spiritual inheritance bequeathed to each one of us, as certain and as real as 'the stars coming nightly to the sky, the tidal wave unto the sea', and which no one, nothing, can deny us, for it is our very being, our breath of life, our spirit, our soul.

We must however, accept full responsibility for the way in which we respond to this 'inheritance', remembering that it is only our own deliberate ignorance or refusal to believe in its existence that can estrange us from it, therefore denying ourselves the opportunity to reach our full, glorious potential.

The author Ursula King in her book, *The Search for Spirituality*, explains to us that; 'spirituality is not an end in itself, but rather a means for transforming ourselves and the world.' It is 'connected' with our life at every level and affects our relationship with everything else, while another author has expressed spirituality as 'wisdom for living'.

Connecting our life at every level and affecting our relationship with everything else. How many times must the question have been asked, 'What *are* we, the real you, the real me?' – not the physical you and me but the 'all encompassing, ethereal, deeper than deep, eternal, spiritual you and me'.

Focusing on our spiritual side (although it is now generally accepted that to be truly happy and balanced we must learn to harmonise both the spiritual and the physical), and thinking in the altruistic, moral sense, is our spirituality a loving, caring and sharing with all life, to put it in its simplest form? To put it on more personal, practical ground, is it when we work on strong, positive feelings that grip us? Something telling us, guiding us; a sense we have, and that we just *know* is more than the physical; or is it when we *feel* the physical giving aid to what we are doing or feeling? But the reality is the 'me', my spiritual side, setting it all in motion.

(Because of *my* thoughts or feelings, such and such a thing is being done by *my* physical side.)

Is 'spirituality', your whole 'being', reaching out in sympathy, to a complete stranger as they recall sadness, suffering, whispering the deeply touching words 'now I know what it is to have a broken heart'? A poor strayed animal; listening to a piece of music that for no apparent reason affects us in an unusual way; words that at another time would not have moved us but here we are almost sobbing at their resonance.

All these signs prove the reality of the spirit and its ability to impress itself on the material side of life, and as we begin to awaken to the reality of our spiritual nature, and the possibilities it holds, so too do we become more sensitive, uncovering a new 'depth' within. We begin to register, perhaps as never before, things we have thought about in an earlier chapter; the meaning and the reasoning behind coincidences, unusual occurrences, dreams, premonitions, déjà vu, and all the other vagaries life has to offer. We begin to see the signs, feel the strength, of a power we know to be far greater than ourselves; a power that we know will never let us down or forsake us; a power to which we can give the name 'Universal Energy', 'Life Force', 'Creator', 'God', or simply, 'our father'…

Having reached this stage on our spiritual path, we are now beginning to understand the true meaning of the words, 'leaning on the invisible'.

• • •

On 25th July 2008 a huge hole appeared in the fuselage of an airbourne passenger plane, a Quantas flight travelling from Hong Kong to Australia. Miraculously, a disaster was avoided, the plane making a safe landing in the Philippines.

It was reported that the passengers appeared to be calm throughout the ordeal, but later told interviewers that they were 'terrified' and turned to 'fervent prayer' for help.

• • •

Becoming aware of our spiritual nature will begin as early as in childhood, although we will not have an understanding of it as such. Innocent, trusting and impressionable, without previously held opinions or ideas, as a blank page we move forward, exploring everything within reach. Marvelling at what are (at this young age) opportunities, endless possibilities for grasping joy and love from all areas of life equally; sensing the mystery, the magic of 'contact'; trust in the ultimate goodness of the world and of all life – expressions of such, as seen in the drawings and paintings of even very young children, never fail to surprise. Children find extraordinary ways to alert us to their inner thoughts and feelings; worry, sadness, feelings of 'joy', 'wonderment', sheer happiness; gurgling with delight, finding immense pleasure in the company of 'imaginary' friends, often spirit children. (Two families returning from a combined holiday in Spain quizzed their four young children as to why they hadn't used the playroom, and were aghast at their reply, 'Because it was full with the other children; they didn't want us.' The parents knew there were no other children in the house.)[2]

Harold Sharp, well-known and well-loved healer, medium, writer, philosopher, now passed to the other side of life after a full and long life of service to others, tells of becoming aware of spirit when he was seven years of age. 'An old monk would frequently appear sitting in the armchair by my bed, seemingly deep in thought or meditation. I always felt happy and comfortable in his presence. As far as I can remember, he never spoke to me during those nocturnal visits. Occasionally a choir-boy came and sang – but not so frequently as the monk.' Harold Sharp, at the age of twenty-one years, became seriously in contact with the monk, whom he came to know as Brother Peter and, through a series of incidents and extraordinary encounters, he realised that this 'wise man' (the monk) was to be his life-long guide and companion on the spiritual path he finally chose.

As we look around the world, and to our own country, we see many signs manifesting, proving to us that, to survive, humanity needs to move onto a higher, more spiritual vibration, i.e. way of life. A traditional researcher into spirituality explains that as this happens, more children will be born with their spiritual gifts intact. As more emphasis is placed on teaching 'good citizenship' in schools, including to the very young, so are children being taught to respect all life, bringing forward what the new curriculum guidance calls 'mini-beasts', bees, ants and worms. Apparently the classes are part of the 'animals and us' section of the primary school curriculum, encouraging children to become 'active citizens' by learning that 'other living things have needs' and they (the children) have responsibilities to meet them.

Children growing up, and inevitably, as for all of us, have life's hard lessons to learn. Suddenly experiencing deep anguish as we feel betrayed by that special little friend; worried by the reverential tones of grown-ups as they mouth the word 'dead', but followed by 'gone to heaven', we have our first serious impression of angels – 'all things bright and beautiful'. Immediately, comfort and reassurance flood through us, our little world is 'steadied' again, all is well.

Have you remembered any particular incidents or incident that happened to you as a child that you might like to record at the back of the book? Did you have a so-called imaginary friend or perhaps a vivid dream that has stayed with you, or do you remember being especially worried about something and will never forget the strange way things finally worked out?

Jack was two when his daddy died suddenly and unexpectedly. One night, now a three-year-old, his grandma sat on the bed beside him, and as she sat there, telling him a bedtime story, she noticed his attention was focusing on something behind her. Finally, she asked him, 'What is the matter?' He answered that there were two people in the room, and one was his daddy.

Church bells that rang out a childhood refrain sung to a young one by her mother comforted her as, suddenly taken away from all she knew and loved, heartbroken, the bells peeling out that same childhood refrain, lulled her into a blissful sleep.

There are children who might feel the flutter of an angel's wing softly brush against their cheek as they say a bedtime prayer. See a bright light that seemed to become 'luminous', significant perhaps to some situation, but the words unknown at that age to describe it. Strange, magical things that happen to us as children but only to be often 'scorned' by the adults, not understood, treated as 'fanciful', ignored, forgotten.

'This is my secret and it is very simple: that which is really important is hidden from the eyes...' [3]

Those words, from *The Little Prince*, a wonderful parable for all ages, end with the little prince telling his newfound earthling friend that he is returning to his own planet, far away among the stars, but, not to be sad as he leaves his body behind; *'I shall look as if I were dead; and that will not be true...You understand...It is too far. I cannot carry this body with me. It is too heavy. But it will be like an old abandoned shell. There is nothing sad about old shells...'*

• • •

Finally leaving the innocence of childhood behind as we step into the grown-up world of materialism, with all the stresses it entails, we feel we must conform to this grown-up world, so often devoid of sensitivity, altruism, caring, love. So often we lose the sense of 'spirit', embraced naturally in childhood; yet still, if we care to listen, having a 'knowing' of that ever present small voice whispering to us 'No' when we make a bad move, or shouting out to us 'Yes', when we hit on a right solution. Lessons of life we must all learn; and all part of an 'on-going' curriculum.

• • •

One night when I was saying my prayers I suddenly felt a great light all around me and I seemed to be walking or rather floating up between rows of figures towards something of intense brightness, and a voice said, 'Go your way in peace and your ways shall be shown unto you.'

But the light was like nothing on earth, it was all around and uplifted me with an indescribable feeling.

Since that day I have not worried about any decision I may have had to make, as I have known that the way that has opened for me has been the right one and always will be.[4]

• • •

The dividing line between a material inheritance and a spiritual one has probably never been more marked or pronounced than in the case of the young Francis Bernadone. His is a life so full of intense drama and greatness that it has been well chronicled over the centuries, in fact since the very time the almost unbelievable events occurred. Francis, one of seven children, was born into a rich merchant family in Assisi, Italy. Assisi is a small, sparkling Umbrian town set on high ground in central Italy, twelve miles east of Perugia. His father Peter was a cloth-merchant, extremely wealthy and wholly intent on making money. He was away in France on business when Pica, his wife (originally from France) gave birth to Francis in 1181/2. She wanted to call him John, but when his father returned home from France, he insisted that his son was named 'Francis', after the country he had just visited.

To be the son of rich parents is not always easy, and Francis grew up used to enough money to spend recklessly and frivolously as he pleased. The story goes that he carried a small bag of gold tied to his belt, as he caroused with his friends every day. Francis was the leader of the young group. They organised drinking parties and nightly brawled their way through the narrow, cobbled streets of Assisi. One historian asks the question, 'Was Francis a Mediaeval layabout?' With so much money he could do just about whatever he pleased, and so it could be no surprise to find him and his friends drifting aimlessly about town, hanging around street corners, getting into trouble. Although Francis could outdo the rest in excessive drinking and despite his superficial life at that time, his wild extravagance shows no sign of 'meanness' in his nature. He was generous, giving presents right and left and he never regretted what he had given away.

'One day in his father's cloth warehouse, in a busy moment, he brusquely sent a beggar about his business and suffered immediately such remorse of conscience that he resolved in future to turn down no plea for help. Open-handedness was second nature to him from his earliest days and he maintained it throughout his whole life.' [5]

Francis lived the life of carefree amusement and ostentation until he was twenty-five and then, as we have considered in this book through other lives, unexpected events happen that can change everything. (Remember reading about Jim Irwin, the eighth man to land on the moon, who was said to have heard God whispering to him at the foot of the Apennine Mountains on his return, and left NASA (the National Aeronautics Space Administration) for the church) Unexpected things happened in the life of Francis. Events occurred that changed his life forever.

He fought proudly in a war between Assisi and Perugia; he was taken prisoner, and spent a year in captivity. On his release, he was a sick man. Making a slow recovery, Francis no longer sought out the noisy, now seeming to him 'empty' activities of his friends. He was restless, fighting a real torment of spirit. An inner change was taking place; his new way of life was beginning.

'The change lasted a long time but progressively took clearer shape until at last his associates realised that Francis had become a different man. He himself experienced his inward tumult as 'a change from bitterness to sweetness'. He felt that someone stronger than himself had taken hold of him and was amazed at his own new attitude;[6] at last recovering full health, Francis wandered dreamily around the little town of Assisi asking himself, 'What gives my life a meaning?'

· · ·

One Sunday last October (2009), I invited a few friends over for a drink on the following Friday and said I would just put a pizza in the oven for a bite of supper. After putting the phone down I thought, 'Oh I wish there was a pizza place near here that delivers,' and as I was actually thinking this, I heard a leaflet being pushed through the letter box, advertising a new pizza place, just down the road – That Delivers!

The following week I was in a taxi, chatting to the driver, a complete stranger to me, and a few miles into the journey, simply to make conversation, I asked him where he lived. He answered, 'One second,' then, pointing straight across the road, and with such a sound of amazement in his voice, said, 'Right there.' We were at his very door!

· · ·

Wandering around Assisi in this dream-like state he now found himself in, Francis unexpectedly met a man with the dreaded disease, leprosy. He had always had a horror of this disease, barely able to look at those afflicted by it, covered in weeping sores and with wasting limbs. The disease also carried with it a nasty smell that made Francis want to run away as fast as he could – but not today. Today he stood his ground. He greeted the poor man, and in his empathy with him, and his strong feeling of compassion, gave him money. He kissed him, touching the leper's hand with his lips, without the slightest fear of contagion. Gradually he began to help in the nursing of even the most repulsive victims of leprosy, in the lazar hospital, near Assisi. This experience probably set him on his first serious step on the road towards his new life, a new life that would see him renounce all worldly wealth and ties, devoting himself entirely to God, living a life of poverty, and striving always to be of service to others.

His second experience, that confirmed the path he had chosen, happened as he was deep in prayer in the half-ruined church of San Damiano, again just outside Assisi. As he prayed before the crucifix, the figure on the cross spoke to him, 'Francis, do you not see that my house is in ruins? Go and rebuild it.' Suddenly seized with violent trembling, Francis agonised, 'Was it imagination, a dream, or a vision? But he knew it was none of these; it was a direct order from God.

Having set about collecting stones and mixing mortar, he rebuilt the little church, soon to realise that the words had meant a rebuilding of the church but not in the material sense; a rebuilding of it to its spiritual vocation; to revitalise, revive its purpose, reaching out to all in need, the poor, the suffering, the lost, the oppressed.

Finally, taking a vow of poverty, Francis publicly renounced his material inheritance, much to the anger and disgust of his father, and set out on a life of the severest hardship, often sleeping in caves and even a hole in the ground, and with no idea where the next bite would come from. He was the poorest of the poor, having now renounced his great material inheritance for the spiritual one he embraced and embarked on; he became a light in the world; a man of exemplary vision and compassion, a soldier of Christ, a champion of all living things and almost certainly, the best known, and best loved, of all the Saints. He was Francis, Francis Bernadone, who became Francis, Saint Francis, of Assisi.

• • •

Have you ever wondered why it is that in the company of certain people, you feel uplifted, positive, even light-hearted, happy! Have you a memory of someone you came across in life, maybe a nurse, a teacher, a neighbour, a complete stranger, a friend, and you always want to 'sing their praises' for the way in which they helped in a situation? For the way they 'cared', and gave unstintingly of their time (most precious), far beyond what was expected of them? Is this the spiritual side of the person being revealed as, forgetting 'self', that person strives to help in whatever circumstance? What about the thousands, millions of people, throughout the world, who sit at a certain time each evening, linking in, to observe the 'healing minute'; selflessly sending out thoughts of light and love to the less fortunate citizens of our planet?

• • •

Margaret adopted Ollie, a little black and white cat, from a rescue home, when he was one year old. She 'loved him to bits' and her parents often worried about how she would react if anything happened to the little cat. Time passed, and Ollie was Margaret's best friend and sole companion after her parents died.

After having him for nineteen years, Ollie died and Margaret went to pieces. She put a framed photograph of him up in her home, and later, noticed a sort of shadow appear on it, as if in the background; as if another cat was there. Margaret couldn't help but feel how strange this was and wondered what it could mean.

Months later, on Ollie's birthday, looking out of the window, she noticed a movement on Ollie's chair, a chair she had kept for him at the top of the garden. There she found a little black and white cat huddled up…straggly, in poor condition, just as Ollie had been when she took him in.

Doing her best for the little cat, gradually, after a few days, she coaxed him into her home and took him to the vet. He had awful injuries, but he has stayed with her and is so loving, she wonders if Ollie has guided him to her for love and protection, and to be her friend, as he had been.

• • •

Is being spiritual, taking the time, making the effort, even risking a threat of prosecution – and all at your own expense, as you dig up small areas of public land in the centre of town to plant vegetables, for use by the community?

This has happened recently in at least one small town in England, where a few people, concerned by the state of our ecology (and threat of possible future food shortages), have answered the call to, 'grow your own'. Taking along a number of young people in the process, who are delighted to be involved, and maybe for the first time, doing something to help others (having a purpose), they have now added a few rose bushes to the vegetable plots, hoping to give pleasure to any passers-by.

(People remain basically the same, no matter in which century they have lived, and it is with a big smile that we read of a little school in Victorian England, way ahead of its time, where the children were encouraged to cultivate their own plots at home, this following on from lessons in the school garden. On their own initiative, without permission, and without the knowledge of any adult, they decided to brighten up the village. Discreetly digging around areas by the side of the road, above cart tracks, and in other, 'public places', they planted flowers in every direction! Imagine the amazement of the villagers as, in due course, they stood staring at the transformation; the whole place alight, ablaze, with colourful blooms.) [7]

• • •

Leaving Christmas behind, and now well into the New Year of 2010, Church Officials and retailers are in unison in their belief that the global economic downturn has been a major factor in encouraging people to rethink their direction in life; re-evaluate their aspirations. Sales of religious Christmas cards soared, as it seems, shoppers preferred to celebrate the true meaning of the festival, forsaking the glitzy, jokey cards with designs that have little or no relevance to the Nativity story. Selfridges showed that sales of traditional cards were up by thirty per cent and religious themed wrapping paper up twenty per cent on last year. Many parents are also choosing biblical names for their children, with Thomas, Daniel, Joshua and James all appearing in the top ten boys' names for 2009…(Rachael and Rebecca being very popular for girls.)

With this trend to perhaps a more serious, deep-thinking attitude to life, there is also apparently, an increase in the number of people attending church. Christian charity 'Tearfund', has said that more than a quarter of British adults now attend church at least once a year. Fifteen per cent say they go once a month – an increase of two per cent on last year (2009).

Ben Wilson, spokesman for the Church of England, commented: 'The economic downturn is perhaps challenging more people to ask questions about where they can place their trust.'

Those words, 'more people asking questions about where they can place their trust', are a good lead into a recent interview, in a magazine, by reporter Jon Wilde, with tough-guy film star Mark Wahlberg. Wahlberg has a tattoo resting over his heart with the words, 'In God I Trust.' Having just finished making the movie *The Lovely Bones*, a chilling story of the brutal murder of a fourteen-year-old girl, Wahlberg's behaviour as he met the reporter seemed to indicate that he had immersed himself more deeply in this role than any before. 'I've put myself through emotional torture making this movie; it's taken me to unimaginably dark places.' Later in the interview, he continued, 'I've never been daunted by a script, but as soon as I realised what *The Lovely Bones* involved, I really had to think about whether I wanted to go to that dark place every day during filming. Every day I'd get down on my knees and pray for all parents who'd lost children.'

Mark Wahlberg talked about his tough upbringing, the youngest of nine, growing up in the poorest Boston neighbourhood of Dorchester. His father left home when he was ten and he became a troublemaker. Dropping out of school, he started experimenting with drugs; his life of crime began with street fighting, stealing cars, then into drug dealing and robbery. But he never blamed his upbringing for his wrong-doing. 'I was taught the difference between right and wrong at an early age. I take full responsibility.'

At sixteen, high on drugs, he was part of a gang that embarked on a robbery spree, leading to a term in prison.

• • •

Marianna, a German lady, tells the experience of a sea-captain, also German, who refused to believe that there was anything after death, or anything at all in stories of 'dreams' and 'ghosts' and 'premonitions' and the like.

Until, that is, something happened at sea. Something happened that shook him rigid, changing his disbelief into one of awe and wonder.

Out of a perfectly calm sea, with not a cloud on the horizon, and with not even a ripple in the water for warning, a gigantic wave appeared from nowhere crashing over the whole ship; sweeping over it as though there would be no tomorrow. The captain logged the event.

Later, he discovered his mother had passed away, at exactly the same time.

• • •

Determined to escape his life of crime, Wahlberg knew he had to 'first of all' learn to stay on the 'straight and narrow'. A Catholic, he dutifully relied on the guidance of his parish priest,

Father James Flavin. 'He was the one person who never gave up on me,' says Wahlberg. 'He was always there for me, through the good times and the bad. Back then, there were more bad times than good. But he always had faith that I could change my ways. He was the first to recognise the actor in me!'

Eventually turning his life around, he found fame and fortune in a pop-star career before his acting breakthrough in 1997 finally established him as one of Hollywood's more versatile actors. Now living in a palatial residence in an exclusive area of Beverly Hills, with his wife and young family, Mark Wahlberg certainly hasn't forgotten where he came from. He regularly visits his old neighbourhood as part of the 'Mark Wahlberg Foundation' he set up in 2001, with the aim of creating opportunities for local children. This 'Foundation' takes up most of his spare time and he is totally committed to it, on a 'day to day' basis. (Interestingly, the new film, *Avatar*, has been 'officially declared', the highest grossing film of all time, and a newspaper headline states, 'The Spiritual aspects of *Avatar* lead audiences to return for more'.)

• • •

Trying to find our own spirituality (you and me, and you *are*, as previously mentioned in the book, if you are still here with me now, reading this); making contact with it and *trying* to live by it. It seems that there are, after all, many more of us seeking the spiritual path, a more spiritual way of life, claiming our spiritual 'inheritance', than we at first imagined.

Another celebrity moving away from being a 'hell-raiser' (his own words) to leading a more spiritual way of life, is the sixty-four-year-old actor, Martin Shaw. He told an interviewer on Radio 4 that he gave up heavy drinking long before he starred as tough guy Ray Doyle in *The Professionals*. 'In order to be an exciting young actor, it was good to be a hell-raiser.' Apparently, he stopped drinking completely in 1970, seven years before the first series of *The Professionals*. 'I discovered a spiritual path which is still the centre of my life, which involves, teetotalism, meditation, and so on. It was like a light of understanding, and I stopped drinking overnight.'

• • •

'It was like a light of understanding.' Ringo Starr, of Beatle fame, recently spoke of how he had been looking for 'enlightenment' for over forty years. 'Being on this quest for a long time, it's all about finding yourself. For me, God is in my life.' Ringo appeared in a documentary about the world's religions last year (2009) called *Oh My God*, in which he declared, 'God is Love.'

• • •

Jim McCloskey, the Divine Detective, featured in Chapter One, gave up a successful business career at the age of thirty-seven to do outreach work in a local prison. Feeling the great need of those who had fallen on hard times and who had no one to turn to, he knew that God had called him for a special purpose. From that moment of his calling, he devoted his life to the service of others.

• • •

A man, who had been a market trader for years – and a popular one at that, one day, 'out of the blue', told Steve, a customer, that this was his last day at work.

Astonished, Steve didn't know what to say or think, but was even more astonished and quite speechless when the trader confided in him that he was leaving to join a monastery, where he hoped to become ordained as a monk

• • •

A Jewish Rabbi gave a congregation the following saying; 'Three factors are necessary to make a life significant. They are God, a soul and a moment.'

Someone, really impressed by the words, interpreted them as; 'The three factors are always present, but not always the recognition...The "moment" is the moment of "recognition", and that may be one, or one-half of a second, but it will illuminate a whole lifetime and never end.'

(The moment of 'recognition' is the moment of 'truth', which could come to us in any manner or situation, or simply in one, unexpected second of 'recognition'.)

Spirituality, our spiritual inheritance, within each one of us, is always there waiting to be called on. Hoping for the chance to lead us in the only way we have of reaching our full potential; leading us to where we will be able to pursue our own best individual pathway; find our own particular way to happiness, truth, fulfilment, in life.

Ballerina Uliana Lopatkina, the principle ballerina with the Kirov in St Petersburg, acknowledges: 'The spiritual condition of a ballerina is as important as her physique. I never dance just with my body.'[8]

Thus acknowledging the truth of what this book is all about; the fact that we are (whether we like it or not), all of us, spirit here and now, inhabiting a physical body;

we are spirit...here and now!

• • •

An American lady, Pat, recalls for us a memory of the way her husband Mathias – passed away some years ago – communicated with her while she was on holiday in Switzerland.

It was in 2004 when Pat, on a tour of Switzerland, feeling a bit 'wary', 'As I had never done such a thing before, in Zermatt one morning, I decided to take a walk-about by myself. I was just about to enter the church cemetery when I said to Mathias,

"If you can, let me know you are with me, it would mean so much to me. I miss you so."

'I turned the corner to the cemetery path and there, in front of me, was a beautiful stone with the name "MATHIAS" on it.

'It is not unusual for him to answer my requests in one way or another from time to time.'

Pat ends the telling of her experience with the words, 'I don't believe in coincidences.'

• • •

The story of the lost city of Atlantis has been around since 355 BC and the controversy as to whether it is fact or fiction continues, although in present-day thinking the tendency seems to be leaning towards 'fact'.

Atlantis suggests an ancient, highly evolved civilisation, which had ships and aircraft powered by a mysterious form of energy crystal, the Atlanteans being extremely technologically advanced. They had wealth beyond measure, living in a futuristic, 'high luxury' society that gradually became even more 'grand' and powerful and hedonistic. It was perhaps inevitable that it would become 'suffocated', wallowing as it did in its own absorption with power, and greed, and total selfishness. It became a decadent society. It became too 'clever'.

According to one of many writers who follow the same theme on Atlantis; 'Atlanteans started valuing material wealth above goodness – that's where they went wrong.' The ancient Greek philosopher, Plato, said of them;

'The portion of divinity within them was now becoming faint and weak so there occurred portentous earthquakes and floods, and during the course of one day and night the island of Atlantis was swallowed up by sea and vanished.'

There is an old saying, 'we are allowed to do so much', get away with so much, go so far, meaning; 'go on, do well, prosper, achieve, aim high', but in the process, 'don't forget yourself'. In other words, don't ignore your principles, that sense of goodness ever within you, your conscience; the small voice whispering 'no' when we are about to make a bad move, shouting out to us 'yes' when we hit on a right solution. Don't forget the magic to be found in caring and sharing; caring and sharing with all life on our planet; the brotherhood of man; personal responsibility.

The thought is being promoted, in all the chaos, the turmoil of our time (now); with financial crises at our door; with threats of such enormous ecological change almost upon us, floods, earthquakes, future food shortages, that we are being 'saved' by a power far greater than any *we* could ever muster. It is moving in, slowly but surely; 'saved' by, as 'has been forecast for centuries', a spiritual revolution; where society, turning from a greedy 'me' attitude to life, will consider 'all life'. Here we will become truly happy, in the forgetting of 'self', as in selfishness, while moving towards a more spiritual philosophy, a philosophy where we will see both our physical nature, and our spiritual nature, in harmony, one with the other.

And how will this spiritual revolution come about? It appears to be that we are moving into what has been called the Fifth Dimension which, to put it simply, means; 'the earth plane lifted spiritually on to a higher vibration, with the consciousness of people turning to a more spiritual outlook in life, instead of focusing so much on materialism'. This new 'awakening' of our spiritual nature, in the twenty-first century, forecast so long ago, being the saviour, 'not only of the planet', but also being the means of enriching our own personal happiness as we move to feeling a more 'connectedness' with others, and with *all* life, in love and in service.

• • •

Science has proved to us that our world, the whole universe, is a far stranger place than we ever imagined it to be. (Being familiar with terms such as vibrations, the aura, etc. you might find it interesting to read that 'an electromagnetic field is a region of influence; every time you use your toaster, the fields around it perturb charged particles in the farthest galaxies ever so slightly.)[9]

Human beings – we're back to you and me – are thought of as the greatest, most complicated, but the most perfect of all creation! Made up of the magnificent physical beings we are (physically necessary for our life on earth), our spiritual side is adventurous, fun-loving, intriguing, esoteric, ethereal, and able to take ourselves on journeys to anywhere if we so choose; to great heights of happiness, to aid, to comfort. Once delved, the spiritual will take us on the adventure of…'one? lifetime'.

• • •

Have you any thoughts, any comments about this chapter you would like to add at the back of the book? A question you would like to ask, and it **will** be answered (test this) in one way or another, in time! Writing is very therapeutic, so 'give it a go'. Maybe you have a few words of wisdom you would like to set down, a memory perhaps, or a – 'coincidence'?

When all is 'said and done', as we 'review' the number of experiences we have covered in this work; as we consider all we have touched on and perhaps related to in our own lives, thinking about 'our own pathway'; how to find it and how to 'get onto it', is all about going 'into the quiet (into the silence' if possible). Going within and within and within.

'What lies behind us and what lies before us are tiny matters compared to what lies within us.'

Going within and within and within to gain a sense of self worth.

Within and within and within knowing our spirit to be our true self.

Within and within and within to find powers of which we are normally unaware.

Within and within and within to bring the real self forward into daily life.

Within and within and within, reflecting, thinking, listening, 'open-minded'.

Going within in the stillness, within in the quiet; within and within and within.

To repeat the words of the little prince;

'that which is really important is hidden from the eyes...'

Chapter Five

Healing; preventative and alternate therapies, conventional medicine, miracles

> 'When we concentrate totally on either the inner realm or the outer reality we limit the scope and richness of our lives.' [1]

A LITTLE BOY STANDS, HANDS on hips, feet together; crosses his feet placing little toes together; bends his knees, body forward; lifts his heels then floats down to a sitting position without using his hands, landing like a feather!

A good party piece, as seen on a TV advert, and an exercise – akin to yoga – in learning how to concentrate; the little boy, in performing this 'party piece', is setting himself up to having an understanding of the way, one way, to leading a good, healthy lifestyle.

The emphasis now, in medical science, seems to be moving towards the promotion of preventative procedures, emphasising the importance of a suitable diet, fresh air and exercise; still thinking along these lines, there is now also a strong realisation of the benefits of yoga, meditation, reiki, reflexology, and the many other tried and true practices in alternative therapies. While with the general recognition of the connection (the need for the harmonisation) of mind, body and spirit as being essential to good health, we are back to what has been known since the beginning of time, Plato being emphatic about it in his teaching in the third century BC.

> 'The cure of the part should not be attempted without treatment of the whole, and therefore if the head and body are to be well, you must begin by curing the mind; that is the first thing...for this is the great error of our day in the treatment of the human body. The physicians separate the soul from the body.'

Plato and Socrates, the Greek philosophers, leaders of thought, gave it as their opinion that it is a mistake in the treatment of illness to separate mind and body because each has influence over the other.

Remember the words of the old song, 'All of life's a Circle': these are words that ring true today as we witness a return to old ways, old remedies, old thinking; and seeing this happening, in our world now, right in the middle of an 'explosion' in the constantly changing scene of 'high technology', is awesome. How can someone, adept at texting, e-mailing, computer literate, with high tech business and visual aid skills, perfect at multi-tasking, find meaning, significance, in lighting a candle, burning incense, want to 'hug a tree'? But they do!!!

Works of art are now accepted as part of the healing process in some of our hospitals. Giant wall paintings brighten lives and help recovery.

In children's hospitals, massive wall paintings are helping the children to become absorbed in something. Singing is a good form of speech therapy, and exposure to the arts, along

with medical care, often sees patients needing less pain relief,
suffering less anxiety, and out of hospital sooner.
Arts benefits are proving to be cheaper for the NHS and
healthier for patients.

The old saying, 'we all do our best when we are happy' – here marking the influence of the mind – is being reborn in the way we are turning, slowly but surely, from the 'shout aloud' materialism we are all immersed in at the moment. We are looking for more simplicity, tenderness, true love (in whatever way you care to interpret those words), listening for the guidance of our higher self, the real, often hidden, you, the real, often hidden, me. Things are turning full circle, if we will only take time to see it.

(It was amazing, watching scenes unfolding, this week, in April 2010 – before our eyes on television, as news came in of a dreadful air disaster in which many of the top leaders of a European country were wiped out, on their way to mark the anniversary of horrendous atrocities performed against their country, years ago. Atrocities still remembered with bitterness, the two countries involved, apparently still sworn enemies, until this disaster changed things dramatically. The 'hated' country, responding to the disaster in such a pouring out of sympathy, sorrow, and yes, 'love', was moving and inspiring to see. Even news commentators talked of a 'healing process', as they witnessed the unbelievable change of attitude by the perpetrators of past crimes who, so warmly, and with apparent great sincerity of feeling, embraced mourners, desperately wanting to share in their loss.

A serious rift between two countries, a rift that has lasted for centuries, is now perhaps, not so serious. The healing process has begun.

'It was December 2009, and two sisters sat, one at each side of the bed, holding their aunt's hand as she passed away.

The sisters lived completely independent lives, but that night, they both had the same dream. They didn't talk to each other about it, but told other people, and it was only later when it all came out that they discovered they had both had the same dream/ experience, each in their own home, and on the same night.

In the dream, they were holding their aunt's hand. She seemed to be going away from them but was very reluctant to go, continuing to hold onto their hands. Then slowly, she moved away, crossing moorland, travelling over beautiful countryside, but it wasn't until they saw (still each in their own dream), a picturesque, old, white cottage, that she hastened away from them towards it, and disappeared.

• • •

Things turning full circle. The film star Sarah Miles, perhaps best known for her films *The Servant*, and *Ryan's Daughter*, always open and sincere about her spiritual beliefs, in an interview with the *Sunday Telegraph*, said, 'Forty years ago I was talking about healing powers and dolphins.' She is here referring to the now proven therapeutic experience of swimming with dolphins. 'Now everyone agrees it's the right thing to do. Everything comes full circle.'

'What goes round comes round.' The village in England where the community is expressing reverence for their ancestors, lovingly gathering ancient bones found scattered in the area and re-burying them with celebration and dignity; the local paper printing the headline 'What's Going On!' A recent survey of people's shopping baskets showed that bottled water is the greater preference over all other drinks. What *is* going on?

With a strong return to appreciating the value – in more ways than one – of old crafts, and the use of natural materials, we also see an interest in old health remedies that are both natural, and maybe don't need the processing and expertise and cost of the pharmaceutical industry. Simple remedies, for sure, but ones that can be very effective.

Perhaps the first remedy we will have ever known, is the comfort and love found in a pair of healing hands as, usually, 'mother' (but anyone who has the 'feeling', the sincere intent, to give care and comfort) rubs a leg or tummy, or gives a big hug. Placing our own hand on our brow or other troublesome area can be a means of self-healing, alleviating discomfort, and we can maybe 'feel' the heat coming from our hands, often a sign of healing taking place; and how about wrapping our arms around our body as a way of giving a self-hug. As the advert says, 'You're worth it!'

(Animals, known to be experts in the art of self-healing, 'lick' their own wounds or sore spots, instinctively knowing how to cure themselves and their young.)

A pat of butter with sugar, rolled into a little ball like a sweet, melts down the back of the throat, immediately easing the soreness. Honey and vinegar used in an assortment of ways for a variety of problems have proved to be effective, with honey itself being a natural antibiotic. Many people swear by the remedy honey and cider vinegar, for arthritis, believing that it clears toxins from the system; porridge can relieve depression, oats are full of vitamin B, vital to the nervous system. Dry white toast helps alleviate diarrhoea; walnuts, believed to help the nervous system, may also lower cholesterol. The Aloe Vera plant is a soother for cuts and sores, Camomile tea is soothing for indigestion, honey in camomile tea is good for encouraging sleep; garlic is good for high blood pressure, colds and flu, and rubbing the crushed leaves onto the skin is a known cure for a verruca...the list goes on and on. Have you any thoughts on such remedies? Perhaps you have a few of your own you could – you know the procedure – *write down at the back of the book.*

Sitting quietly somewhere warm and comfortable, undisturbed, where you feel at ease, meditating (more about this later), 'day-dreaming', or dozing, is a great reliever of stress, and of course another effective self-help remedy is to be 'optimistic'!

Are you the sort of person whose glass is always half-full?

The Healing Buddha teaches:

> 'By stimulating and directing positive, joyous feelings we can change the essence of our inner patterns and experience. When positive or joyous feelings and attitudes pass through each organ and circulate throughout our whole system, our physical and chemical energies are transformed and balanced.'

Transformed and balanced. Here again we have the message, the message of the importance of being 'in harmony', mind, body and spirit. Mind is the consciousness of the spirit. (Consciousness: awake, aware, intentional.)

A new medical investigation, launched into the study of NDE (near death experiences) includes the placing of hidden images in hospital bays, which can only be seen from the ceiling, looking down. Dr Sam Parnia, leading the investigation, explains that it could be a way of proving whether patients are really looking down on their bodies from above, in a NDE, as they often report on what they see while having this experience. The naming of 'hidden images' is hoped to be a foolproof way of gaining yet more evidence on this phenomenon, experienced by countless people.

UK hospitals participating in this experiment include

Hammersmith, Southampton, Birmingham, Swansea, Edinburgh and Cambridge.

The healing power of music is tried and true. James Orent, violinist and conductor of the Newton Symphony Orchestra in Massachusetts recently conducted the orchestra in a programme entitled *The Healing Power of Music*, which included talks by music therapists, medical researchers, stress management experts and alternative therapists. 'I know of so many people who have been helped through serious illness, psychological issues and family losses by their attachment to music,' says Orent.

We must all have experienced at some time the upliftment felt by listening to a particular piece of music, perhaps a 'stirring' at the sound of a brass band, and wasn't it a solitary piper who roused an entire army to victory with his plaintive strain, when all appeared lost? The enthusiastic, heart-felt singing of the crowd at a football match has been proved to help a team to victory. The crowd raises them to higher and ever higher endeavour with the thrilling, if sometimes, raucous, sound; and who cannot fail to, maybe have a tear in the eye or a lump in the throat, at a rendition of the firm favourite, the old hymn tune, 'Abide with Me'?

A family approached James Orent, after a performance where he was guest conductor of the Boston Pops, to let him know that classical music had pulled their fifteen-year-old son out of a coma; and as they were able to reach him, in that way, through music, he is now eighty-five per cent back to normal. They stressed to James Orent that 'music had brought him back to life'. Songs can apparently stimulate memories and brain functions in Alzheimer's patients, and songs are known to decrease anxiety, blood pressure and heart rate.

· · ·

A distressed cat managed to find its way to an animal rescue centre, even though it had its head stuck in a tin of cat food. It wandered into the SPCA centre in Middlebank, Dunfermline, where the can was removed.

'No damage was done' said Colin Seddon, the manager of the centre, 'and she was very pleased to be freed from the discomfort that comes with having your head stuck in a tin can.'

• • •

Ways of self-healing are many, and often so obvious that they are 'ignored'. Going out into the garden, visiting the local park; having a laugh – the expression, 'if we don't have a good laugh at least once a day, it is a wasted day', proved to be true; reading, meeting up with a friend for a chat, a good old 'chin-wag' as the saying goes.

Thinking (positive thoughts), praying with sincerity.

There is healing for us in our choice of colour, both in what we wear and in how we decorate our homes. Colour is a powerful influence on minds and emotions. Colour is a vital force.

'In the truest sense of the word *colour* is life. Our very thoughts and feelings vibrate to colour and our auras are throwing out bright or dull colour-tones continuously. The power of colour is so important a fact in our lives that modern medical science is showing an increasing interest in colour-therapy – a subject which the ancient Egyptians studied and practised![2]

To give just a little thought to the meaning of a few colours (and we are not looking here at the variation in tone, which will alter the meaning to a certain extent, such as lighter or darker, cloudy, bright): *rosy pink,* the symbol of unselfish love; *orange,* the symbol of energy; *yellow,* for mind and intellect; *green,* the symbol of harmony and sympathy; *blue,* for inspiration and devotion; *violet,* the symbol of spirituality.

The science of colour is fascinating, and with it the wonder of why we have a favourite (colour), and how that favourite can give an idea of the sort of person we are, and how the colour, or colours, around us – our aura – change in accordance with our mental state, and our physical state. How often have we heard people say, 'I thought I would wear such and such a colour today, to 'brighten myself up'; 'never wear black when you visit someone ill in hospital'? Colour therapy; yet another way in which we can help ourselves; definitely worth thinking about and even acting on!

The healing power of crystals has been known, and used, throughout history, no less so than in our twenty-first century, where they are appreciated for both their healing qualities, and for their beauty. Each stone can emit a certain type of energy, having a beneficial effect on our well-being. It is now common practice to find a person, male or female, slipping a citrine crystal into a pocket or handbag for support during a certain ordeal they may have to face. Citrine raises self-esteem and is good for overall emotional well-being.

♦ Blue Lace Agate can give a sense of courage, and help in discovering the truth;
♦ Carnelian gives a good balance and connects you with your inner self, giving good concentration;
♦ Aquamarine, a good soothing stone said to pacify nerves, helping to promote calm and tranquillity.
♦ Aventurine is also good for calming anxiety and fears, while Bloodstone can help in decision- making and intuition, also known to help purify the blood and clear toxins.

Again, the list could go on and on.

• • •

Years ago, a Tyneside Piano company, Retailers, Restorers and

Repair Specialists, moved their workshop to an old, disused 'Methodist Church' that was in Shields, on the Tyne.

One night, the proprietor, Barry, locked up, made sure all was secure, as usual, and headed for home.

Later that night, he received a phone call from the police.

They reported having had a phone call from a child saying they were locked in the workshop and couldn't get out. The police, thinking it could be a hoax call, kept the child talking while the call was traced, finally going to the place – but no child could be found.

Barry was certain no one was in the workshop when he locked up; the police equally certain it was no hoax.

Years later, Barry's son, another Barry, was about nineteen at the time, at the same premises and talking to his dad on the phone. No one else was in the building. Suddenly, he heard the tinkling of a piano, immediately went to investigate, searched everywhere, but there was no one to be found.

Barry knew he had heard the sound of a piano playing and so did his dad, on the other end of the phone.

• • •

Wondrously, just as animals are known for their ability to 'self heal', so too do they reach out to the human society also sharing their planet, healing naturally through an outpouring of unconditional love and devotion and loyalty, often when no one else is there to heal or care.

Our 'humanity', so often in past times and present, not including the animal kingdom, which we determined to 'dominate' and 'destroy' and treat with the most barbarous cruelty.

And – yet – stories abound; ever popular stories, eternal stories, reverberating through history and still happening today, in now time, telling of the courage, the intelligence, the determination, of creatures there for us in a time of need.

Boz five, and Mickey three, two Jack Russell terriers, stand proudly together, heads held high, as they pose for a newspaper photograph with the heading, '2 dogs save their injured owner with long cuddle'.

Michael Dyer slipped and broke his neck in two places when he tumbled down a thirty-foot slope at a remote beauty spot near Brixham, south Devon. The dogs kept him alive by cuddling up to him for sixteen hours overnight, 'until he was found by a walker, who thought he had stumbled across a body'.

'As Michael lay slipping in and out of consciousness,' the newspaper reported, 'in temperatures that fell as low as 7c (44f), they kept his core temperature high enough to stave off hyperthermia and keep him alive.' He also fractured an elbow against a tree that broke his fall. Michael, whose dogs are everything to him, especially since the death of his wife, told how he managed to let them off their leads to get help, but they refused to leave him.

• • •

Animals are there for us in our time of need; how many people have found companionship and love in the company of an animal – even a tiny bird – sadly making the comment, 'the only true pal' they have. The idea to take animals on visits to homes and other 'care' establishments has been around for a long time and has proved to be a most successful form of therapy for residents (and staff) alike. Stroking an animal is a known and accepted way of releasing stress.

The Times newspaper reports that the US army, in a growing concern about the human toll of combat stress, fighting wars in both Iraq and Afghanistan, are increasingly using horses and dogs in the treatment to rehabilitate traumatised veterans; previously an option for those with physical disabilities. 'We're using dogs a lot for patients with invisible wounds too,' said Lieutenant Colonel Matthew St Laurent, assistant director for occupational therapy. 'They have a tremendous effect.' His department started using dogs in 2005 as 'comfort animals'. The Lieutenant continues, 'Dogs are extremely responsive and their love is unconditional. Petting a dog is very soothing.'

A new programme, a voluntary organisation, to set up homeless animals with traumatised service veterans in the Washington area is apparently hugely successful. One soldier at the shelter, picking a Jack Russell terrier called Xena (partly because of a plaster cast on her paw), saying, 'I walk with a cane and I'm injured too, we're both healing together.' The dog is attending therapy with him.

• • •

During a radio programme discussing the role of protestors against land development, particularly in the green belt area, and areas designated to be secure for the preservation of nature, the question was asked, 'How can we put a price on nature?'

(On the back of a card for the RSPB: 'Love nature; celebrate every crawling, hopping, buzzing, fluttering part of it.'

How *can* we put a price on nature, and how can we put a price on love? On the unconditional love, the healing love, and on all the benefits we receive from the animal kingdom.

The haunting picture of a gorilla, tenderly holding the body of her dead baby, which she carried around with her for over a week, is poignant enough to make even a hardened heart 'cry'. Visitors to the zoo at Munster, in Germany, were in tears at the sight of Gana, so grief-stricken by the sudden death of her three-month-old baby, Claudio, that she refused to give him up. Instead, she cradled and stroked the lifeless little body, carrying it with her everywhere, on her back.

Apparently, such behaviour among gorillas is quite usual. 'In the wild, a mother can keep hold of a dead baby for weeks, and there is even evidence of gorillas trying to 'bury' their dead, by covering the body with leaves.'[3]

. . .

'Things were not happy for either of us. Each in our own circumstances, going through a worrying, desperately sad, and anxious time. And so, it was in this 'frame of mind', that I tried to reassure Pauline, my close friend, that we were not alone. That our loved ones, who had died, were still with us. I kept saying to her, 'they are with us and they will be listening now, to this conversation'. My father used to say this when any departed ones were mentioned, 'Yes and they will be listening'.

Trying hard to comfort and convince her, I kept repeating that they were still with us 'and they will be listening now'. As I said this, I thought to myself, 'Well if they really are, I wish they would do something to prove it, like flash the lights or something. Immediately on this thought, one of the lights on the chandelier near me 'flashed'. I nearly ran out of the door!

. . .

Animals feel sorrow and pity; they can communicate pleasure, and pain; animal minds have the intelligence, according to one branch of science, to sometimes out-do human evolved brains; in other words, human evolved brains are not always as good as animals...

Humming birds can detect a storm coming; starfish can grow a new arm; starlings can try things to improve; baboons expand their social network; elephants know all about the whereabouts of other elephants; bees have many skills and are caring parents. Chickens are quite clever; and how about the little dog patiently waiting the return of its owner, knowing exactly when the time draws near, even though it varies considerably, with no set routine.

There is now a proved understanding of the parallel between human lives and the animal kingdom.

Jenny Smedley, in her book *Pets Have Souls Too*, explores the powerful bonds and communication that exists between the human and animal worlds, in both earthly life and spirit. She tells of telepathic pets having extrasensory perception and psychic abilities. She recounts tales of spirit pets who revisit their owners after death; guardian pets who appear in times of danger to protect their owners, and pet messengers who bring messages from the spirit world.

• • •

As 'spirit' (and remembering that we are all of us spirit), only now we also inhabit a physical body necessary for life on the earth plane. As 'spirit', we are part of all nature, proudly taking our place in the order of things; hopefully raising our consciousness and behaviour in such a way that we can live on a far higher level of happiness and purpose – looking to, and appreciating, earth energies to sustain, to give inspiration for life, for healing – as did our ancestors. We look to our brothers and sisters (as St Francis called them) in the animal kingdom, our 'friends', as sharers in this magic that is creation.

'Everything here for a purpose, a purpose in everything'; life, within the guidance and love of spirit, full and rich and omniscient and free, encompassing 'everything'; every crawling, hopping, buzzing, fluttering, and human part of it; eternal; seeing death, in the words of one elderly travel writer, as simply another horizon…yet another horizon…simply another horizon.

Harold G Koenig, a professor at America's Duke University Medical Centre, has concluded that spiritual values are good for you.

The professor is quoted as saying: 'People who feel their

life is part of a larger plan and are guided by their spiritual values have stronger immune systems, lower blood pressure, a lower risk of heart attack and cancer, heal faster and live longer.'

A television programme featuring alternative remedies, focused on 'hypnosis' as the first in the series. In this startling, yet serious look at the practice of hypnotherapy, a patient was to have her front teeth extracted and implants inserted, all done under the influence – with no other procedure, not even drugs, used – of a hypnotist.

The programme started with Anna, a woman bored with life, telling how she was tired of going to work, then home again, and no other excitement coming her way, responded to an advert to find a suitable patient for the programme. After a number of visits to the hypnotherapist, Anna was chosen to be the most suitable patient, seeming to respond naturally to the method.

Weeks later, came the actual operation, all done with cameras rolling, an interviewer standing by, 'dentist' and 'hypnotist' and a full medical team at the ready to step in if the procedure faltered, or failed.

It was 'nerve-wracking' to watch, unique and astonishing. The patient going easily and confidently under the control of the hypnotist and remaining so while the extractions took place, the implants inserted.

It was a 'hold your breath' sort of programme where 'seeing' is 'believing'. To think that such an operation could be, and was performed, without any drug or anaesthetic being used, with the minimum of fuss and procedure, all under the influence of a hypnotist is amazing.

• • •

'Healing' has always been 'there', performed and named in

accordance with the time in which it was practised. Looking back to the Middle Ages, and beyond, there is evidence in records of such, both in the written word and in pictures, and we need look no further than to the Bible where we have some of the most wondrous stories of healing ever told, performed by the greatest healer of all, 'Jesus'.

A stained glass window in Canterbury Cathedral, the shrine of Saint Thomas Becket, portrays scenes of healing in the Middle Ages, featuring a child in bed and people with diseases, including leprosy. The scene shows the way of thinking at that time when there was a great belief in prayer and in healing. The church dominated the lives of the people, religion was everything, and it was the church that helped to protect the sick and the poor, until seemingly, it lost its way and 'over excessively' tried to imbue its influence on the population.

Many of our alternate remedies today were 'practised' in those far-off times, under different names. To look at just a few:

Reflexology: the ancient Egyptians practised this art, the oldest known artefact depicting reflexology being a wall painting found in Egypt in the Tomb of the Physicians dated to 2330 BC.

The Chinese, Indians, Incas, and American Indian Tribes such as the Hopi and Cherokees of North Carolina practised reflexology, which is based on the premise that constant energy flows through ten channels, or pathways, referred to as Zones.

These zones link all organs, glands and structures in the body, the organs and structures being reflected on the feet and hand in miniature, like a mini-map (of the body). Reflexology, commonly used to soothe and relax, can also provide stimulation. Reflexology is understood as being excellent for helping circulation and for eliminating waste products in the body, and for giving help with other conditions such as migraine, depression, backache.

• • •

Trish and Sonya, working in the evening at 'Simply Food & Drinks', in Carlisle, were startled when a strange white mist appeared on CCTV screens showing the outside of the store. The mysterious 'mist' drifted in and out of the store about ten times in an hour. Trish told the local paper, 'I've never believed in things like ghosts, but until somebody can explain to me what it was, I believe now.' Customers coming in and out of the shop were staring at the screen, fascinated.

One theory is that a spirit has been disturbed by workmen renovating a flat across the road which was said to be haunted.

Trish explained that before they saw anything she felt as if she was freezing down her right side. She remarked, 'It's going to happen again,' and it did.

As the night goes on, the mist becomes a brighter orange, seeming to acquire more of a definite figure.

Now the locals are wondering if there is a logical explanation or if the 'orange mist' could really be a spirit manifestation.

• • •

Meditation can reduce stress and combat depression, and its popularity is on the rise. 'Just take ten minutes out of your day to do a simple breathing technique and you will see big results.'[4]

For many years now, meditation has proved to be a highly successful health therapy approved by the NHS, the Mental Health Foundation now advising the NHS to routinely prescribe it for depression. Scientific studies have shown that meditation is at least as effective as antidepressants (and with none of the unpleasant side effects).

Andy Puddicombe, meditation guru to Premier League footballers, cabinet ministers and leading actors, gained his wisdom from several years as a Buddhist monk. Setting up Headspace, a not-for-profit organisation, his guiding principle is to provide simple meditation opportunities for as many people as possible presenting it as a life skill. 'My message is that meditation is not necessarily about sitting on the floor cross-legged and chanting for hours. I say to people, just take ten minutes out of your day to do a simple breathing technique and you will see big results.'

The various techniques used in meditation are numerous, and the acclaim given to this procedure, this life skill, is unanimous, in that the benefits, now starting to be 'recorded' scientifically, in a serious way, are colossal.

TM, or Transcendental Meditation, was brought to this country in the sixties by the Maharishi Mahesh Yogi, the method becoming famous almost overnight when taken up by the Beetles, who even visited India to practise it under the guidance of the Maharishi.

At a 'Change Begins within' concert held recently in New York, Paul McCartney talked about the experience of TM. 'It was a great gift that Maharishi gave us,' he told a press conference. 'For me it came at a time when we were looking for something to stabilize us toward the end of the crazy sixties. It's a life-long gift. It's something you can call on at any time. I think it's a great thing it's actually coming into the main stream. It interests me that an ancient cure may be the solution to a modern problem.'

Ringo Starr added that he 'meditates a lot, sometimes. It's a gift he gave us.' (the Maharishi)

With TM, again it does not have to mean sitting cross-legged on the floor chanting a mantra for hours at a time. TM is so easy, so effortless, it can be practised on a train or bus or in a busy airport.

Dr James Le Fann, writing for the *Sunday Telegraph*, stresses the overall benefits of regular TM. 'Science has now shown that deep relaxation, such as in meditation and yoga can change our bodies for the better.'

To think that ancient cures may be the solution to modern problems!

Marylebone Health Centre, opened by The Prince Of Wales, in a church crypt in 1987, was the first NHS practise to use such complementary therapies as massage, acupuncture and homeopathy.

Faith Healing carries with it the need to believe, to have faith that a healing process is taking place. (Animals don't have faith and yet they can still be healed.)

Magnetic healing is a transfer of energies from one person to another.

Spiritual Healing is defined as a form of healing the body physically or mentally, by means of prayer, laying on of hands, or quiet meditation. Spiritual Healing where, through the concern, the compassion, of one human being for another, a transmission of healing energies can take place; the healers allow themselves to be a channel for the healing intelligences in the spirit world, a transfer of the necessary energy flowing from spirit through the healer to the patient. Spiritual Healing is now an accepted part of life, with new evidence of its success emerging almost daily.

Under a newspaper headline: 'Healing experiments defy explanation says scientist', we read that doctors and researchers at American universities are discovering further scientific proof that hands-on spiritual healing, or 'energy healing' in its various forms, undoubtedly works.

Avoiding use of the name 'God', or universal energy, or life force, can we simply say that the 'something else' factor must come into the equation, before true healing can take place? The 'something else', which perhaps is triggered off by the whole-hearted sincerity, the depth of compassion, the 'kindness' of the healer?

In a lecture in Swansea, at the Academy of Psychic and Spiritual Studies, entitled 'Why Kindness is good for you', Dr David Hamilton explained how the expression of kindness, compassion and gratitude directly affects the chemistry of the brain, the nervous system and heart. He stated, 'Positive thought and kind emotions generate health-giving and cardio-protective roles. They help to multiply the body's important hormones which strengthen our immune systems and make us feel good.'

• • •

As a little lad, Dan used to visit the home of the insurance lady every week with his mother, to pay their dues. Over the years they became very friendly and he called her 'Aunt Minnie'. Often going in for a cup of tea and a chat, Dan especially enjoyed the visits because of Daisy, her little spaniel. He loved watching Daisy; the way she would jump up onto the back of the settee to have a better view out of the window. This was her favourite place, and Dan was always amused at the way you could tell she didn't miss anything going on in the street outside.

Aunt Minnie took Daisy everywhere with her, and it was some years later when Dan – who hadn't been visiting for a while – called on this particular day with his mother. They knocked on the door as usual and both were surprised at no reply. 'Strange,' said his mother, and with that Dan gave an extra big bang on the door, looked through the window, saw Daisy sitting in her usual place on the back of the settee, and turning to his mother said, 'I know she's in because she would never leave Daisy in on her own.'

Dan was the one who changed colour when his mother told him the dog had been dead for some time.

• • •

In the January 2000 edition of *Prevention* Magazine, leading medical practitioners were invited to give their predictions for future developments in alternative medicine. Among the predictions offered were that energy medicine would be a major development in the next century, and we would learn to harness the power of the mind, not only to heal, but also to scan the body to locate disease.[5]

Having long understood the importance, the necessity, of energy, for our comfort and for progress on this earth plane, at last the world is waking up to the fact that everything is made up of energy. We humans are pure energy, both physically and spiritually. In accepting the reality, the power of 'natural' healing to be indisputable – instructors and students of an ancient Indonesian martial and healing art, aim to develop the skill of using their internal energy, to heal themselves and others. In accepting the power of natural healing to be indisputable, whether it be through self-healing, or crystals – each crystal emits a certain energy which can have a beneficial effect on our well-being; or spiritual healing, or colour therapy, or 'thought'; 'by stimulating and directing positive, joyous feelings we can change the essence of our inner patterns and experience'.

(When positive or joyous feelings and attitudes pass through each organ and circulate throughout our whole system, our physical and chemical energies are transformed and balanced.)[6]

In accepting the indisputable truth of healing, we are also expressing a belief in our own spirituality.

At a NHS Hospice: a leaflet for adults, and babies, with stomach problems, suggesting a visit to a qualified chiropractor (baby tummy massage given.)

It appears to be that spiritual healers, to add to their knowledge of training and development, are being encouraged to utilise 'more complex energies' – energies that may be able to affect physical matter, and energies that healers are just learning about, learning how to detect. It is probable that there are many more (energies), so far undetected or unimagined, that we could call on, and it is a popular concept that the source of some of these energies could be the spirit world.

Have you seriously considered any of the alternate remedies mentioned so far, or had any of the treatments? If so, perhaps you would write your own thoughts on the experience, record what is your favourite colour, and note down how you feel when wearing it; or if it is a colour in a room, does it enhance your feeling about that room?

You are not superstitious at all, never have been, but there is one thing you would do if you encountered a certain situation (such as not walk under a ladder). Why would you do this, is it by way of protection, or luck; what do you think?

You have *never* had a 'so-called' paranormal experience, *never,* but, on thinking about it, there – was – one – incident, where you… . Why not record this incident at the back of the book, if you haven't already done so?

Say we are made aware of (for whatever reason) a little more depth to a certain situation in our lives than we had at first thought; it could be an incident involving a seemingly trivial, casual remark. Looking at the incident more carefully, and after thinking about it, seeing it in a different light, with even a tiny glimmer of new understanding, we are changing our pattern of thought. Slowly but surely we are opening our minds to other possibilities, maybe to the truth that things are not always what they seem.

A trivial or casual remark can be a cry for help; a joke hiding a depth of sadness we cannot even begin to comprehend; a casual remark baring a soul needing a friend; or a casual remark can be, of course, simply a casual remark.

Does it not seem to be that what we are really lacking in this, the start of the twenty-first century, is 'understanding' – understanding and sincere care and concern for each other? (We hear more and more from authorities, obviously worried about our state of affairs, asking for more co-operation and involvement from society as a whole.) Is it that we need more understanding, sincere care for each other, and for the world? In other words, is it that we need a little more 'spirituality'?

The word 'compassion' is heard often enough, as is 'care', and we all know the expression, 'tender loving care', abbreviated to TLC as used in hospitals and care-homes, but in modern living, have we not slipped a little down the spirituality league? If we have, then how can we remedy this? If each one of us show a little more care and understanding for others as we go through life, both in the way we think (remembering that thoughts are living things), and in the way we act, by maybe saying 'I will think about you' to someone we know is going through a bad time. They will remember your words, and those words will help them. They will remember your words and, 'hopefully', remember to pass them on to someone else they may meet up with, who is in need of that bit of extra support. The 'pass it on' method works! Why not ring that person you know who has a lot on their mind and they are alone, or poorly and alone, or simply, alone…just to let them know that *somebody* cares. Pass it on.

• • •

Jimmy was on holiday in Tenerife when he received news from home in England, that Dennis, his close friend, had been rushed into hospital with a suspected brain tumour.

A devout Catholic, Jimmy immediately prayed, sending out strong, positive thoughts for Dennis and made his way to the local Catholic Church to light a candle for him.

Every day for a week, Jimmy visited the church, praying and lighting a candle for his friend.

On the day that Jimmy couldn't get a candle to light, his anxious thoughts were 'Oh God no! Is this a message?'

He later learnt that Dennis had died at that time. At the time he couldn't light the candle.

• • •

Miracles happen every day (for instance it is a miracle the way that bones knit together naturally), and certain things defy explanation.

Lee Hadwin is a man from Zimbabwe who has wandered around in his sleep since the age of four, drawing pictures with anything he can get his hands on. He draws on walls, scraps of paper, anything, but he can't draw at all when awake. His is a rare case that has interested doctors and psychologists around the world.

At the age of fifteen he started to make more intricate drawings, little crosses and squares making a beautiful mosaic, a portrait, and so on. One doctor said, 'It is just part of the sleeping pattern,' but...?

This 'night-time' wandering can happen three or four times a week then nothing for a few weeks. After such a strange night's escapade, he wakes up with migraine; this lasts for about fifteen minutes.

With this great level of curiosity in his condition, a video was made showing him asleep, then getting out of bed, drawing on walls – even though he leaves paper out now! He draws very fast, at an incredible speed, and galleries are interested in his work.

He himself thinks there is something deeper with him, on a universal level. He thinks there *is* a greater universe out there.

Is it that he taps into a different dimension in his altered state of consciousness (sleep) – remember the tale of Isabella Macleod meeting up with Princess Diana? People studying physics are particularly interested, looking for answers to it all.

A man from Belgium, forty-six years old, has lived in a coma for the last twenty-three years, after being involved in a car crash.

Completely paralysed, not able to move at all, he could not make anyone understand that he was conscious; only his mother believed that he was. Trapped in his body, he could see, hear, feel everything, but could not move. 'I knew what I could do but no one else did.'

Recently making a breakthrough in his attempt to communicate, at last making people realise that he is conscious, he explained that he 'meditated' to pass the long years, adding that he is an optimist.

New technology has shown that his brain is 'working' as it should.

A large lottery grant has been awarded to a medical charity for research into the benefits of healing provided by 'The Healing Trust'.

The sum of £205,000 has been awarded to Freshwinds, a Birmingham medical charity, which will work in collaboration with the university and a Birmingham hospital.

Miracles happening every day; a German medical student, one of a party of medical students, visiting various places to witness all types of healing, called in at a healing session in a Spiritualist Church. The healer was working in trance. Tom Lawrie, the healer, always worked (in trance) with a German doctor from the other side of life, a Doctor Romano, who 'took him over', in the trance state.

Tom Lawrie was an ordinary, north-country man who devoted his life to helping others, and his belief in 'the other side', knew no bounds. He spoke no other language than his own. The

German student talked to Dr Romano (Tom Lawrie in trance), speaking in German, and received a convincing reply.

• • •

Lourdes, in France, perhaps the most famous of all the Holy shrines, witnesses healing on a daily basis. Being 'immersed' in the healing waters of the 'Bath' is especially amazing. Given a 'bathrobe' to wear, having stripped down to your underwear, you join a queue of people also waiting to be 'immersed'. Your turn comes, and on entering the 'bath-room', held at each side by an attendant, you are gently lowered into the water, to then step out and into the changing room, by now completely dry.

Lourdes: the place where – through endless prayer, through 'love energy' from the masses who congregate there made up of people from all over the world – great and unbelievable healing has, and does, still take place; and it all began, as these things so often do, in the humblest of circumstances.

Bernadette Soubirous of Lourdes, was the eldest of five children whose hard-working parents had fallen on difficult times, and she took her share in the struggle to help the family survive, working partly in the house, and partly in the fields watching the sheep.

Hardly able to read or write, Bernadette suffered from several childhood illnesses, which left her weak and asthmatic, and small for her age. From a very early age, however, she showed that she had immense faith in God, and when she was 'chastised', because she was unable to learn her catechism, she quietly answered that at least she would always know how to love the good God.

On Thursday, 11th February, 1858, when Bernadette was fourteen years old, she was collecting firewood at the foot of a hill where there was a small cave, or grotto, where cattle often sheltered. She was with her sister Marie-Toinette and Jeanne, a friend.

Marie and Jeanne quickly kicked off their wooden shoes and

walked across a little stream, looking for deadwood, leaving Bernadette behind, hesitating because of the cold, and stopping to take off her stockings. As she did this, she heard what sounded like a strong wind. She looked towards the cave where, to her utter astonishment, she saw a figure in the opening – the figure of a Lady of small stature and incomparable beauty.

The Lady was 'surrounded' by light. She looked towards Bernadette as if wanting her to come nearer. She put out her hands, a little away from her body, and on her right arm could be seen a rosary with large white beads on what appeared to be a golden chain. Although frightened, Bernadette did not want to run away. Experiencing a mysterious attraction, Bernadette took out her own rosary and started to recite the prayers. The vision lasted about quarter of an hour, then, quite suddenly, the Lady disappeared.

• • •

'For as long as I can remember I have had the feeling that there is an unseen hand guiding me. My husband and friends often hear me say jokingly, "My guardian angel is watching me." I do not have an explanation of this feeling but I have a constant experience of calm.

'Two years ago, my grandmother died. After her death I had a sense of her being with me. Shortly after, driving my car to work, I crashed into a tree. It was misty, and I must have entered a sudden blanket of fog.

'I received serious internal injuries, and later was informed that the doctors did not think I would live through that day. However, I had an operation. I remember no pain. I remember feeling comforted all the time.

'Towards the middle of my stay in hospital I was aware of a face looming over me, a face with a gentle smile. Suddenly my grandmother came to me, she kissed my eyes and told me I would be all right. She took my hand and started to take me up. We reached a fence, which we did not cross. I could see clearly the other side and could tell anybody about what is was like.

'Another form came to me, an uncle of my husband's, who died the year before. This time he took my hand and told me it wasn't time yet. We went down and I woke up. I struggled to keep awake, but lapsed again into sleep and my grandmother appeared again and the procedure was repeated.

'On awakening the second time I managed to keep awake, frightened and convinced that the experience was not a dream and was not the influence of drugs.

'None of my family are church-goers. We were all christened Church of England. I have felt drawn to the church from an early age and I still attend. I feel a deep compassion towards sick people. I realise, logically, that my outlook could be the result of my Christian feelings. My experience in hospital could have been the result of my binding to the church, it could have been drugs, it could have been a dream.

'The experience is lodged so vividly in my mind that I prefer to believe that I did experience this happening. It has strengthened my belief in God and life after death.

'I work and have a responsible job. I say this to help show that I am in no way a religious fanatic.'[7]

• • •

The vision experienced by Bernadette, of the beautiful Lady standing at the entrance to the cave, was the first of eighteen apparitions that took place over the next few weeks, sometimes with many people present, many out of curiosity.

During one of these visions, the Lady asked Bernadette to drink at the spring and wash in the water, although there was no spring to be seen. Bernadette scratched away at the earth's surface and found water rising, which she was able to drink. (This spring was soon yielding 27,000 gallons of water a day and occurs, even today, and in times of drought. The spring has been channelled into a reservoir from which the 'Baths' are filled and there are twenty drinking fountain heads.)

During her seventh appearance, the Lady instructed Bernadette to ask the priests to build a chapel by the Grotto (cave), and this is at the heart of Lourdes today.

Suffering against a background of enormous opposition and disbelief and personal chastisement, Bernadette pursued her mission to help the Lady who had appeared to her; opposition and disbelief that such miraculous events could have centred on a young, poor, uneducated girl. With a final acceptance from the authorities that the Apparitions were genuine, and the Lady who appeared to her – and at the fifteenth appearance disclosed herself as the 'Immaculate Conception' – the whole idea of Lourdes was developed into the Holy Shrine, the Healing Centre that it still is today.

Franz Werfel[8] points out that death extinguishes a human face in the twinkling of an eye, but death illuminated the face of Bernadette. Bernadette's body remains incorrupt and can be seen laid in a glass reliquary in the Convent of St Gildarde in Nevers, France.

• • •

Suffering, in whatever form it takes, and whether it be martyr, saint, or ordinary people like you and me, takes its toll both mentally and physically.

Suffering strips a soul bare, leaving a dark stain not easily removed except perhaps, through time, to change to a 'lighter hue'.

Through suffering, we reach out to something 'more' than our physical minds can comprehend, but through suffering, 'know' is there.

Suffering takes us to a place where no other person can join us, where no one else can 'be', except at a time of 'their own (personal) suffering'. But through suffering, in this dark and lonely place, we gradually move onto a higher consciousness; in this time of great despair, separating ourselves from 'ordinariness', drawing on all our inner resources, we take on the mantle of understanding; and in this new understanding and open-mindedness, we touch on 'the way'. We follow the natural, eternal part of what it is to be human; looking towards what is good, what is right, what is true, knowing ourselves to be spirit, children of the Universe, a living part of God; ageless, timeless, loved beyond our understanding.

In sheer 'joy', in pure abandon, child-like, let us hold our heads high, fling our arms open wide to the Universe, hold a Tibetan prayer wheel (in our minds), endlessly spinning the words 'thank you, thank you, thank you'.

Say a prayer; light a candle; send out *positive* thoughts raising our consciousness to the heavens.

Think happy. Be happy, knowing you have only to ask...

Love nature; celebrate every crawling, hopping, buzzing, fluttering part of it.

Live in harmony, light, freedom, JOY!

Daydream, sit in the silence, meditate; love what is good.

Remember 'the way'.

Tell someone you love them; tell them we are all 'loved beyond our understanding'.

Be Happy, all Love! Love! Love!
Pass it on.

. . .

A little boy stands, hands on hips, feet together; crosses his feet placing little toes together; bends his knees, body forward; lifts his heels then floats down to a sitting position without using his hands, landing like a feather!

A good party piece, as seen on a TV advert, and an exercise – akin to yoga – in learning how to concentrate; the little boy, in performing this 'party piece', setting himself up to understanding the way, *one way*, to a good, healthy lifestyle.

Chapter Six

Does prayer work? (And why do people pray?)

> *'As o'er each continent and island,*
> *The dawn leads on another day,*
> *The voice of prayer is never silent...*

WE CELEBRATED THE WORLD Cup this year, 2010, and England put up such a poor performance that when the coach, Fabio Capella, was seen standing with his hands clasped together as if in prayer, one of the commentators was prompted to remark, 'That might be the only answer.'

Prayer is very much in the news just now. Russia's church leaders are asking people to pray for rain as excessive drought affects the country.

Journalist and author Pythia Peay's horrendous images of the Haiti earthquake followed her and refused to allow her to sleep. The only solace, for herself and others caught up in the tragedy of Haiti was, when everything possible had been done during the day, 'to lay down our burdens at night on the altar, and "let go", and get the sleep we need'. Bringing to mind the simple prayer that has, and still does, help countless people of all – and strangely, 'no' belief: 'Let go, let God.'

The Archbishop of Canterbury asked on the radio, 2009, for

fasting and prayers for the people of Zimbabwee, while a police chief this year (2010) claims the crime rate in his 'home town' has been slashed by praying.[1]

Inspector Roger Bartlett reports that the power of prayer has helped catch criminals, boosted crime detection rates and even reduced the number of people killed on the roads. Inspector Bartlett, who has twenty-three years experience, is 'convinced' that faith work has had positive impact on policing in Barnstaple, Devon.

The most significant answer to prayer, he claims, was a dramatic fall in the number of serious road accidents in North Devon, after he asked a group of local Christians to pray on this issue. He also works with Christian volunteers from local churches. The street 'Pastors', as they are known, patrol towns in Devon at night helping people who need support.

Ian Bartlett's comments, that praying can help police work, were backed by the Christian Police Association.

A reporter for International News, Jane Flanagan, writes about interviewing former Archbishop Desmond Tutu. For Jane, this was a different experience as it was the first time she had been 'led' in prayer by the subject of her interview, 'but Desmond Tutu is in constant touch with God'.

Every day in his office in Cape Town, he begins by praying for all in need, whatever their circumstances in life. Sending out deep, sincere prayers for the benefit of individuals and for the world, he is aware that the democratic South Africa he helped to build is as needful as ever of 'direction and help' from a higher source. He hopes that his forthcoming retirement from public life will provide him with even more time for prayer and reflection.

• • •

Jodie Smith, thirty-one, of Bridlington, East Yorkshire, had a nightmare in which her fiancé, Scots Guard Martyn Brown, in Afghanistan, was shot in the left foot.

She sent a Facebook message to Martyn telling him about the nightmare but he had already set off for the front line.

A week later he telephoned her to say he had been shot in the left foot.

• • •

A new book, *Prayer Energy*,[2] tells us that through everyday prayer we can transform states of mind and ways of living. 'Prayers for guidance, healing, and wisdom for everyone, whether your faith lies in God, the Universe, Mother Earth, the All – that – is, or Divine Creator.'

(Words of advice or help given to someone in need, now often heard are: 'Send your troubles, problems, whatever, out to the Universe; put it out to the Universe.')

To whomever, or whatever, we send out thoughts or prayers in the intensity of despair (and this includes the most ardent of non-believers), it is interesting to find that at the height of our greatest 'trials', we turn *'spontaneously'*, and 'naturally', to this power. To this 'phenomenon' that is the bedrock of what it means to be 'human'.

• • •

Gail Ironson is an AIDS researcher and professor at the University of Miami. In the mid-nineties, when having HIV was tantamount to a death sentence, Dr Ironson noticed that a number of patients never became ill. Dr. Ironson wanted to know why, and the answer she found was surprising.

'If you asked people what kept them going so long, and what kept them healthy, the reply was often "spirituality". It was something that kept coming up in the interviews, and that's why I decided to look at it.'

She studied a patient's relationship with God in an attempt to predict how fast the disease would progress. She measured viral load, which shows how much of the virus is present in the patient's body, and immune cells, which fight off the virus.

Over time, Dr Ironson said that those who turned to God after their diagnosis, had a considerably lower viral load, and maintained immune cells at a much higher rate than those who did not (turn to God).

'In fact, people who felt abandoned by God and decreased in spirituality lost their immune cells 4.5 times faster than people who increased their spirituality.'

Dr Ironson is one of the first researchers to connect a patient's approach to God with specific changes in the body.

But what *is* prayer, why do people pray, and does it work? Everything in life changes; governments, ideas, environment, fashion, style of living, modes of transport, new emphasis on this, new emphasis on that, yet people, basically, don't change. No matter in which century or time they have lived, there has always been the need for prayer, no less so than in this our present twenty-first century.

Science (and it has certainly tried) cannot give us the answer; swathed as it is in academia, and within its own artificial setting, science cannot capture the truth of the moment when a desperate call for help is answered, a despairing soul shown the way. Science cannot understand the 'soaring' of the spirit, for whatever reason; the magical uplift, the transformation that can take place when contact is made with a 'something', usually not seen, not heard, yet a positive presence in a life, just waiting to be recognised.

Eric Clapton, rock star, and even more than that an icon, a living legend, tells how, after yet another heavy drinking session while on tour, having already suffered, as he tells us, 'one or two alcoholic breakdowns', he hit a wall of desperation.

'It was like a moment of clarity when I saw the absolute squalidness of my life at that moment. I began to write a song called 'Holy Mother', in which I asked for help from a divine source, a female that I couldn't even begin to identify. I still love that song, because I recognise that it came from deep in my heart, as a sincere cry for help.'

It wasn't until 1987, a few years later, while in a treatment centre with his visit coming to an end, that panic hit him and he realised that nothing had changed within him; drinking was in his thoughts all the time and here he was, going back out into the world completely unprotected.

'I was absolutely terrified, in complete despair. At that moment, almost of their own accord, my legs gave way and I fell to my knees. In the privacy of my room I begged for help. I had no notion who I thought I was talking to, I just knew that I had come to the end of my tether. I had nothing left to fight with. Then I remembered what I had heard about surrender, something I thought I could never do – my pride just wouldn't allow it – but I knew that on my own, I wasn't going to make it, so I asked for help and, getting down on my knees, I surrendered.'

Eric Clapton continues, very bravely, and very movingly, with his testimony, explaining how, within a few days, something had happened for him.

'An atheist would probably say it was just a change of attitude, and to a certain extent, that's true, but there was much more to it than that. I had found a place to turn to, a place that I'd always known was there, but never really wanted, or needed, to believe in.

'From that day until this, I have never failed to pray in the morning, on my knees, asking for help, and at night, to express gratitude for my life and most of all, for my sobriety. I choose to kneel because I feel I need to humble myself when I pray, and with my ego, this is the most I can do. If you were to ask why I do all this, I will tell you…because it works, as simple as that.'[3]

• • •

Louise Wright, twenty-five, began seeing a ghostly young girl in her flat in Portsmouth (which was in a converted orphanage), who she believes has twice saved her life.

One night she was 'woken' by the spirit after leaving her oven on, and another time felt a strong gust of wind which blew out a fire started by a candle. No windows were open at the time.

Louise talks to the ghost whom she calls Morticia, Morticia telling her she would meet a man called Paul at a party. She did, and at the time of reporting this experience was still seeing him.

• • •

We are 'taught' that prayer is our own, personal, sincere communication with the Universal Energy, the life force, the Creator, God. Praying to a divine consciousness that has our best interests at heart, not always getting what we want but often finding later that what we wanted was not in our best interests anyway. Eric Clapton tells us that he has no problem with religion and he grew up with a strong curiosity about spiritual matters, but his searching took him away from church and community worship to the 'internal journey'. He says that before his recovery began, he found his God in music and the arts and that in some way, in some form, his God was always there but now he has learnt to talk to him.

The internal journey; probably the most important journey we will ever make. The internal journey, often preceded by a 'wake-up call' which touches lives in strange, unimagined ways, playing to each personal need, acting on each individual, vibration. Acted on, resolved, the divine presence witnessed:

'I was absolutely terrified, in complete despair. At that moment, almost of their own accord, my legs gave way and I fell to my knees. I knew that on my own, I wasn't going to make it, so I asked for help and, getting down on my knees, I surrendered.'

• • •

'Alone in my room, feeling extremely desperate about the seeming foolishness of life, I asked out loud, that if there was a God, could He help? I was immediately overwhelmed by the feeling of a Presence/Light/Love, all around; it seemed everywhere, I really can't explain. It appeared to last for a minute or two, although I can't be sure. I lost all sense of time. I was left with an indescribable feeling of peace and joy.'

'This moment completely changed my life. Everything suddenly seemed to make sense. Now, in middle age, I still look back to those few moments as the most real and important in my life. I am firmly convinced in the reality of God (called by whatever name) and the power of prayer.'[4]

• • •

'When I don't know what to do I simply say a little prayer asking for guidance, and it never fails to help me to make the right decisions.'

• • •

'With this final passing, the death of our little dog, I was totally alone in the world; friends, yes, but no one of my own; no one of "my own", to rely on, to quarrel with, to make plans with, to love. And it was now the words of the old hymn "For we have no help but Thee" that came to mind, words in my desperation I changed to "For I have no help but Thee"; words that took over, and became the corner stone of my life.'

· · ·

The internal, spiritual journey, and a Divine Presence witnessed. Does it matter if the divine presence, this 'all encompassing love', is discovered in art, or music? In an answer to prayer, in a child's smile, or in our mother's eyes; in an unexpected act of kindness, or a reading from the scriptures, or a sudden awakening to 'compassion'; compassion for the less fortunate, the sick, the sad, the lonely, the animal kingdom, our planet? Does it matter if we can't understand the meaning of life; can't understand the vagaries of fate with its often cruel twists and turns; why this had to happen, and that? Does it matter if we don't understand the meaning of the Holy Trinity, the sacredness of the mass or indeed the 'mechanics' of any religion?

(We hear that each religion has some of the truth but there are many paths to God.)

Yet always, over-riding *everything,* the questions, the probing, the experiments, the highly respected, authoritative answers, is the fact of mystery, the mystery of life. There is a reason for everything, and we repeat in ever more reverend tones, 'in awe', as we contemplate yet again, the wonder of the whole, great, magnificent, stupendous, astonishing and never-ending Universe, the great truth of which we are all, each one of us, an integral part.

How many of us charge blindly through life not able to see anything more to it than the material side of existence; getting on with the ordinary business of living, and then – something happens? A devastating blow that leaves us 'floundering around' in abject misery, or it might be an unexpected incident that leads to 'who knows what', but again, is devastating. Things happen. We are knocked out of our comfort zone and can't even recognise the 'ordinary' because the ordinary isn't ordinary anymore. We can't focus on what was our 'everything' because it too has deserted. The very street we walk down every day has become unfamiliar, so far removed are we from the 'usual', in this move we have made to another state of consciousness, triggered off by despair, by the traumatic ordeal we are going through.

It is now, often at such a desperate time in our lives when, humbled through circumstance, we might find ourselves calling out from within to a 'something' we have heard about since childhood, ignored, maybe even 'scoffed' at, but at this time, when all else has failed, may show us a tiny chink of light in the terrible darkness engulfing us. Perhaps it is now, at this time, in our own private place, when we will fall down on our knees whispering the hallowed words, 'Our Father', and be thankful that, at last, we have been 'led' on to, the way.

• • •

Montrose Air Station in Angus, Scotland, now a Scottish heritage centre, has long been the target of many strange 'goings on'. The heritage centre is housed in the original headquarters of the former airbase, and visitors have reported strange 'energies' around the airfield; phantom footsteps, doors opening and shutting, the sound of aircraft engines, shadowy figures walking in and out of rooms and even the sighting of a pilot in full flying kit.

The most notorious were the sightings of Lt Desmond Archer of the Royal Flying Corps who was killed when his biplane crashed in 1913, at nearby Lunan Bay. He is said to have haunted the area until honour was satisfied in 1917, when a government inquiry concluded that he had not been killed by his own foolhardiness, but because of poor repairs to his plane. But the latest phenomenon has the experts baffled.

A seventy-year-old valve radio has started making random broadcasts which can last for up to half an hour, despite not having any power, and is not connected to any source of electricity.

The vintage radio set is kept in a re-creation of a 1940s' room.

Several people have heard Second World War broadcasts, including the big band sound of the Glen Miller Orchestra and speeches by Winston Churchill.

Bob Sutherland, treasurer and a trustee of the air station said, 'I have heard it playing Glen Miller. The volume is low but the music is quite identifiable.' Others speak of hearing Winston Churchill.

Volunteer Marie Paton, whose father Jack Stoneman bought the wireless second-hand in 1962, reported, 'It's a bit scary. I thought someone was playing a prank on us until I heard it myself. Technicians who have removed the back of the old radio and examined it have found 'nothing but cobwebs and spiders'.[5]

· · ·

A doctor sat at the bedside of his patient, a man dying from lung cancer. He sat with the patient's wife and children. The man knew that he had little time left and so, speaking in a hoarse whisper, he chose his words carefully. Not a religious man, he revealed that recently, he had begun to pray frequently.

'What do you pray for?' the doctor asked.

He replied, 'I don't pray for anything, how would I know what to ask for?'

Surprised, the doctor thought, surely this dying man could think of *some* request. Pushing him, the doctor then asked, 'If prayer is not for asking, what is it *for*?'

'It isn't "for" anything', was the man's thoughtful reply, 'It mainly reminds me I am not alone.'

Larry Dossey, MD, talks in his book, *Healing Words*, of prayer being our tie to the 'Absolute' (his reference to God), a reminder of our unbounded nature, of that part of us that is infinite in space and time and is Divine. He writes that it is 'the Universe's affirmation that we are immortal and eternal, that we are not alone'.

Recalling that his book is about science and prayer, he wonders why prayer reveals itself in scientific experiments at all, 'but we have seen that it does'. He continues, 'Although science has much to say about prayer, it raises more questions than it answers. The mysteries of prayer not only remain, they deepen.'[6]

· · ·

After more than three weeks trapped in a dark, sweltering mine, nearly half a mile below the Atacama desert in northern Chile, miraculously, contact was made with the thirty-three miners who reported being well, in spite of their dreadful ordeal, an ordeal that could last up to a further three months before rescuers can reach them.

Through pipes, strategically placed down the mine, and a tiny capsule, contact is made and supplies posted. Mario Gomez, sixty-three, who is, it is said, profoundly religious, led the men in regular prayer sessions through the worst of the early days, and when emergency supplies were being 'dropped', Gomez asked for pictures of Jesus and Mary and a miniature Bible. Jaime Manalich, the health minister, has said that they think he (Gomez) has great influence over the group and, 'he's helping us a lot'.[7]

The voice of prayer is never silent, the need to pray evidenced every moment, somewhere, with answers true to each call, quietly infiltrating, leading, supporting, calming every situation; 'a very present help in times of trouble', [8] every moment, somewhere.

There are countries around the world where everything 'stops' for twenty minutes each day at prayer-time; shops and businesses close, cafes empty, as people congregate out in the streets, lanes, car parks, wherever they find themselves, to go down on their knees and pray. This happens five times a day in at least one country.

Rahimullah, in his sixties, lives with his family in Afghanistan where he tends the British Cemetery in Kabul. His prayers are all important to him. He prays five times a day, waking up with the first call to prayer at three-thirty or four a.m.

'When I pray I feel light, and I always want to smile when I finish. If you don't pray you feel heavy.'[9]

• • •

'Every week, millions of people of different nationalities and religions are involved in some form of prayer – with friends and colleagues, in a congregation or alone in the privacy of their own homes. We may each be praying to a different Godhead, using many different pathways, but the whole of humankind is unquestionably linked by prayer in one form or another.'[10]

Millions of people from all over the world link in together every morning at 10.00 am and/or at night at 10.00 pm for the 'healing minute'. They believe that the power generated by this positive act of collective thought will be a light in the world, sending out beams of love and help to the conditions prayed for, while at the same time helping to raise the consciousness of people everywhere on to a more spiritual level.

Everyone is welcome to join in with this 'healing minute', simply set aside the time, whether you are in company or sitting quietly at home, to send out a thought (prayer) for help in a certain situation. It can be a personal prayer or a more general one, say perhaps for the benefit of the world; but to join in will add your 'weight' to the result and has undoubted benefit for all partakers.

Prayer is with us, with each one of us, constantly, whether we are aware of it or not. It is 'there' weaving in and out of our thoughts (a thought subconsciously placed can be received and acted on as a prayer), weaving in and out of our dreams, igniting intuition, perhaps generating a tiny spark in our emotions, sending a message through coincidence. (A thoroughly spiritual man has said that when he prays, coincidences happen; when he doesn't, they don't!)

Prayers are the strongest link between mind, body, and spirit, and the guide of our 'internal journey'. Prayer is our spiritual inheritance.

· · ·

Trevor, a taxi driver, loves reminiscing on 'life' and fate in particular. He especially enjoys re-telling the story of how he and his wife first met. Trevor had booked to go on a much-needed holiday to Cyprus, hoping he would have saved up enough money to make it when the time came. Near the time of the holiday, he realised that he would not have enough money, and had to resign himself to the fact that the holiday was off.

At precisely this time, the syndicate he was in at work had a substantial win, and Trevor found himself with an extra seven and a half thousand pounds. Trevor went to Cyprus.

Meanwhile, his wife Anne, whom he had not yet met, also decided to have a holiday in Cyprus, if she could afford it. She too made plans, booking the holiday but at the last minute found that she could not afford it either. Out of the blue, and quite unexpectedly, her father stepped in and gave her the money.

Trevor and Anne first met one night on this holiday, and it was the start of a romance that led to many happy years of marriage, and yet another reason for Trevor to dwell on 'life' and fate, when he discovered that, after their first meeting, she had told her friend, 'I am going to marry that man.'

· · ·

From being children, many of us will associate 'prayer' with goodness, with the right thing to do, the 'natural' thing to do, and we remember the question, often asked by adults, 'Have you said your prayers?' We understand from being very young that it is important to remember others in our prayers, members of our family, friends, sick children, animals, and to ask God to 'bless our world'. Prayer is part of the inherent goodness that lies in each of us, and, as we move on in life, to whatever age, we never lose that special feeling of oneness, satisfaction, uplift, when we say a kind word, do a kind deed, please someone.

'Kindness is "Spiritual" in action!'

'When I pray I feel light, and I always want to smile when I finish.'

(We spend time thinking about how to connect with our spiritual side – as in reading this book – but we already *are* connected when we 'help', 'care', and 'love'.)

A study by scientists at Mindlab International, based at the University of Sussex, has found that doing good deeds, helping others, can actually improve your health. They say that both psychological and physical health is the benefit of doing good deeds. Helping others increases happiness, boosts self-esteem, lowers stress and reduces anger.

The head of the study, chartered psychologist Dr David Lewis-Hodgson said: 'Put simply, everyone wins. Doing good things for others, with positive thoughts and feelings, has a health benefit to you too.'

'Doing good for others, with positive thoughts and feelings!'

As with 'healing', as with 'prayer', touching on a greater, higher consciousness than the ordinary cannot be explained except by some divine intervention, with positive results, *according to the intensity, the sincerity, the depth of feeling expressed by the supplicant.*

• • •

Air Chief Marshal Lord Dowding, commander in chief of fighter command from July 1936 to November 1940, the time of the Battle of Britain, was a man of prayer. His leadership in the Battle of Britain was acknowledged by Sir Winston Churchill as 'an example of genius in the art of war'.

At a memorial service in Westminster Abbey, he was 'hailed' as 'this man who did so much for our country, to whom we all owe so much.' He was an 'Architect of Deliverance'.

Lord Dowding made two vital contributions to the defeat of the Germans. One, he developed, and had radar coverage provided in the South of England so that we had early warnings of any impending raids by enemy aircraft. Two, he persuaded the war cabinet (he often met with much resistance to his ideas but persisted) against sending more RAF fighters to a defeated France in May 1940.

(We were successful because we had sufficient numbers of fighters available and would not have had if they had gone to France.)

Air Chief Marshal Hugh Dowding, as he was then known, was a brilliant air combat strategist whose belief in prayer, and guidance through prayer, and his belief in the after-life, and whose outspokenness on his 'other-worldly' belief was thought by many to be the reason why, tragically, he was removed from his post without receiving the full recognition he deserved.

(Publication of his book *Twelve Legions of Angels* was 'suppressed' in 1942. The British Government considered that it contained information that might be of use to the Germans; it was finally published in 1946.)

In a speech in Parliament, seventy years ago, when Winston Churchill praised the Battle of Britain aircrews who defeated the Nazi attempt to invade the United Kingdom, he declared; 'Never was so much owed by so many to so few', and it led to those brave airmen being known as 'The Few'.

The man who led 'the few', as head of the British Royal Air Force Fighter Command, was Air Chief Marshal Hugh Dowding.

Believing as he did, in the power of prayer, Hugh Dowding gave credit to any wise decisions he made, in the course of his duty, to this phenomenon. He believed that the key to life, to prayer, is connecting with something we seem to have lost in our secular, materialistic society/age. Through his books, *Many Mansions* and *God's Magic*, to name but a few, he injects his readers with his own wisdom. With his own insight into the meaning of life, his sadness was that in a materialistic age, 'We *feel* the lack of spirit; we must make room in life for our "soul", our "spirit"; to know we are all part of some larger, magical purpose.'

He advises us to 'ask, pray, then follow your own heart, your own intuition, which is God's magic'.[11]

1969 saw the production of the much acclaimed film, *Battle of Britain*, starring Lawrence Olivier as Dowding, and with an all-star cast including Michael Caine, Trevor Howard, Christopher Plummer and Michael Redgrave. Hugh Dowding, who was by now 'Lord Dowding', consulted as he was during the making of the film, which showed that he had received 'unjust treatment' by the 'authorities' of the time, has now, with his full (?) story being told, had his true worth recognised.

His full (?) story told, and his true worth recognised.

Another story circulated at the time, possibly circulated by circles close to Lord Dowding, was that he asked the film makers to give recognition to the important part prayer and guidance (from the other side of life) played in his life. Disappointed at what seemed to him, in view of the film, reneging on a promise, we see the only notable suggestion of the 'spiritual' side of Lord Dowding at the very end, when, however, as is often the case, what is left 'unsaid' takes on 'a significance', an importance of its own.

We see Dowding, as played by Lawrence Olivier, leave his desk and walk out onto a terrace, where he stands, deep in thought, slowly taking his gaze across panoramic views of beautiful

England, calm and green again, sparkling in bright sunshine, the land happy, content, in the certainty that the worst is over, the battle won.

Then, as if to convey a message, he raises his eyes, but only slightly. He becomes as one with the camera as it lifts the scene, soaring gently over 'beautiful England', green and pleasant land, with its history, its tall trees and chimney pots, its courageous citizens; lifting the scene, taking the viewer up and on, ever higher. Up and on, ever higher, until, melting into a cloudless, heavenly blue sky, pausing; pausing long...giving time for reflection...time for a prayer; time for a heartfelt prayer of thanks.

• • •

Some years ago, Susan's son died tragically at the age of twenty-seven years.

Recently, and after much thought, she finally made the decision that it was time to change his bedroom; 'it was time for a change'. She couldn't decide about the colour of the curtains, but seemed to lean towards a beautiful pink she had seen...but then, there was also a turquoise she really liked. Susan struggled to decide, and, at last, almost against her better judgement as she later recalled, chose the pink.

However, even as she was putting them up in the bedroom, she was thinking that maybe she had made a mistake.

At the same time as Susan was deliberating about all this, Margaret, her sister, who knew nothing at all about the curtains, visited a psychic, along with some friends. She was quite mystified and curious, when the message was given to her, 'Tell your sister she's chosen the wrong curtains!'

• • •

To pray is to accept, however subconsciously, that we are more than this physical body we inhabit while on the earth plane, and that although we do have individual consciousness, we are connected to the whole, great (yes, saying it again), magnificent, stupendous, astonishing, never-ending Universe.

Prayer is a friend; prayer is a guide, a 'medicine' that helps to keep us on the right track; prayer is 'the way'.

Author Doris Lessing likens prayer to 'a simple grateful thought turned heavenwards' as 'the most perfect prayer'.

But what does prayer mean to you, if anything? Have you ever had the need to try it, in, say, difficult circumstances, or do you pray as a matter of 'habit'? Perhaps you are someone who, suddenly feeling elated at something wonderful happening, experiences a song/prayer in your heart. Maybe you haven't given it much thought but are now willing to 'give it a try'.

Whatever prayer may or may not mean to you...will you consider it seriously and try a little 'prayer experiment' for a few weeks (or months)? You might even like to note down any feelings or results you have at the back of the book, remembering, as we must all do, that it is the sincerity, the depth of feeling that we pour into our prayers, and our expression of heartfelt thanks, that works the magic.

Notice any specific changes within yourself or your circumstances. Do you feel lighter, brighter, more positive, 'safe'; do coincidences happen more frequently when you pray, and do you find yourself marvelling more and more at the way things 'work out'?

• • •

'I am aware of a "consciousness" outside my own. I sense it...in times of great stress or anxiety when I "pray", sometimes wordlessly, for some way out in intolerable situations. There is always an improvement, or I realise what I must do to help myself.'

. . .

'When I knew my mother would not live many months, I relied on this power to give what help and support I could to my parents, who to some extent depended on me in particular. This I would say I was able to do in answer to prayer – though it was not the sort of daily prayer said on my knees, but an inner consciousness of a supporting strength.'

. . .

'I pray...fairly regularly, not in set words, often not in words at all, but bringing forward ideas – gratitude, guilt, and people whom I wish well and want to help. I derive comfort from handing over these ideas, and get the feeling that they are received.'

. . .

'In times of distress I have often found my own pleas or prayers answered, sometimes by an inexplicable feeling of peace which seems to arise simply from the fact of praying – although I do not know what or who I am praying to.'

. . .

'Being a lonely child, I talked to God as many children talk to imaginary companions, and the habit has remained with me all my life...'

. . .

'To pray is easy – I relax into the Presence, as I call it, and tell my problems or make my requests and leave them there...Petty jealousies and hurt feelings disappear...'

. . .

'Thank God, I had always believed in prayer and knelt to pray for what must have been two hours. There were tears everywhere;

I felt weak and so alone. Then I truly felt a brightness around me and a firm hand on my shoulder; words just can't explain it, but I knew I was not alone. Afterwards nothing had changed. I still had the ordeal to go through, but not alone. I came through it a better person because of it.'

• • •

'Prayer seems a two-way action. I pray for love that I may give more love to my fellow man; and there is no doubt that I receive it in abundance. But the mechanics of the thing remain a mystery.'

• • •

'I say, "Please, YOU, help me to start. Where must I begin?" and somehow – it is as if someone took me by the hand, the way we do for blind people so that they can orientate themselves – I am set in motion. When there is a tricky conversation to start, a new contact, a difficult phone call to make, or when I see lovers or other partners trying to find each other, I say to myself, "Please, Angel Raphael or whoever you are, help me with your presence," and it is a fact that I can easily find the right words, that I manage to put people at ease. Of course, one may say that "prayers" of this kind do nothing else than summon energy within ourselves. But why should we feel so helpless without it or so grateful when we have it?'[12]

Why do people pray? The answer is, of course, because it works.

Chapter Seven

Living with the light

> *Harmony and Understanding*
> *Sympathy and Trust*
> *No more falsehoods*
> *Mystic Revelation*
> *The Minds True Liberation*
> *Aquarius*[1]

TIME, LIKE THE UNFATHOMABLE phenomena that it is, rolls ever onwards pushing through centuries and into millennia as if – there – were – no – tomorrow.

And now, here we are, having just 'crept' into the Age of Aquarius, otherwise known as the Age of Enlightenment, which many believe is the time of the Spiritual Revolution, forecast centuries ago.

If we were interested in Astrology, the study of the stars and the influence they have on human affairs, we might read that:

> 'The dawning of the Age of Aquarius follows the polar axis leaving the sign of Pisces, where it has been for the last two thousand or so years. Jesus Christ is associated with the sign Pisces, the Fish. Many believe

that the entrance of the Zodiacal pointer into Aquarius will herald a time of brotherhood and peace, with the focus shifting from the devotional religion of Christianity to a 'New Age' based on a synthesis of Universal religious principles'. [2]

This 'New Age', still very much in its infancy, in which it is said, 'humanity will move onto a higher consciousness', aspiring to change our way of living to a more spiritual, less materialistic, selfish, society, has been struggling to emerge for a long time. So now, it is here. We are living in The Age of Aquarius, The Age of Enlightenment, evidenced, as we look around us, in a multitude of ways.

Have you noticed TV adverts appearing to be more 'inclusive' than ever, with neighbourliness, caring and sharing, a constant theme; a 'food hamper' advert in December 2010, featuring band and choir singing carols in a village, villagers joining in, and the slogan: WIN it, for you and your neighbour.

During the recent cold spell (weathermen reporting it as the coldest for a century) fear of fuel shortages seemed to be a real possibility. A plea from the authorities read, 'Don't fill up the tank, fill it half full. Leave some for your neighbour.'

A comedian, at the end of his television show, tells a 'good news' story, showed clips from a film, the story of a teenage girl whose handicaps led to her suffering bullying at the hands of other young people. Her release from this ordeal came in the form of a dog, who became her constant companion and friend, getting her out and about, running, playing; in no time her whole life was transformed.

Finally, the comedian asked viewers to send in any of their own 'good news' stories, which he said he will try to 'air'. (For years now, people have been 'calling out' for more good news items to be reported in the media, to give some uplift to life, instead of the dreadful, degrading and depressive news that is continuously fed to us.)

The financial problems the whole world is facing, encourage 'home-based themes' to bring people, the family, together: a super-chain store, offering customers twenty per cent off dining room furniture so that they can 'sit down and eat meals together'; vouchers from the government to encourage 'healthy' eating.

'Cheaper meals for two' advertised, again encouraging people to stay at home.

There is a trend to a more 'open' way of living when you do go out; away from 'lace table cloths, chandeliers', sitting quietly in corners, to an inclusive, friendly attitude; a 'getting together', sometimes with wooden tables, informal, casual.

Well-off people, who don't need their winter fuel payment, are sometimes giving it back to the community, financial worries of the less well-off, inspiring generosity and concern in those who 'have'…

The *Secret Millionaire* programmes where millionaires spend time living with communities, 'incognito', as they try to assess the most deserving way to give money, and the wealthiest of all, the 'Billionaires', Warren Buffett, described as the world's second-richest man – this was in 2006 – announced that he was giving an estimated eighty-five per cent of his twenty-four billion fortune to charity. He planned to give the majority of the money to the Bill and Melinda Gates Foundation, a charity set up by Bill Gates, the Microsoft founder, to fund medical research and educational grants.[3]

Melinda and Bill Gates today (2011), along with others, are living proof of the dramatic turnaround by successful people to help, give back to society, and feeling it is their responsibility as a family to give back.

In 1985, John Paul Getty (the second) gave an interview to Henry Porter of *The Sunday Times* in which he was asked about his enormous generosity to charities and numerous other causes. His has been a life of great unhappiness and great good fortune, but perhaps the 'telling' part of the interview came in his words at the conclusion:

'I believe in God and an afterlife, although I don't believe in tiers of "Cherubim and seraphim". We don't just disappear with death. As long as I have money, I will give it away'.

• • •

It was some months after the death of his dog, Judy, and Derek still missed her badly, grieving for the companionship they had shared for many years.

With no such thoughts in his mind at this particular time, however, as, tired, he made his way home from work, from the late shift down the mine, at about four in the morning. Approaching his house, he remembers feeling no surprise at all as Judy came bounding along to greet him, and as he quite naturally and spontaneously held out his hand to her saying, 'Hello Judy.'

Not so with Judy though. On coming close to him, the dog stopped in her tracks, hair standing on end as if terrified, turned, and fled away into the night.

Derek always thinks of the incident as one in which the tables were turned. Instead of Derek being afraid of seeing the (ghost) dog, she was afraid of seeing him!

• • •

Entertainment in our new age, all encompassing, with CDs of chanting and plainsong by monks and nuns making the charts over the past few years, along with CDs of music performed by 'The Priests', a group of practising Catholic Fathers.

Famous singer, Tom Jones, has turned his attention to a more serious side of life with religious connotations, in his new album,

Praise and Blame. A senior executive at his record company has complained that the tracks on the album sound like hymns, but Jones himself has described it as a return to his roots, as the son of a Welsh miner, growing up in Wales. It is composed of blues numbers and spirituals, with titles such as 'Lord Help the Poor and Needy' and, 'If I give my Soul'.

Through the philosophy of Rapper Kirk Nugent, whose words under the title, 'Signs of the Times' rap out thoughts on the 'New Age Spirituality' (lessons of love, a reminder of our purpose here on earth), we are also reminded that there is 'so much more to life than what we see; we must be concerned for our spirituality'.

In a perfectly suited 'mellow intonation', but with a strong, fast, backing beat, he begs us to listen, see the warning signs before it is too late...

Children of the earth not to lose their way, never to abandon their dreams by chasing nickels and dimes, to sacrifice so much for material gain.

Give service, your time, your love, your talents, back to the community.

You still haven't collectively learnt to love your brother from another race.

Watch for the signs; the ones who think they are running the show are *not*.

——many signs while earth welcomes another paradigm...

Floods, earthquakes, climate change, are just warning shots from the earth, saying, 'I've been loving you way

too long but you are not loving me back.'
Spiritual wealth sacrificed for material gain.

Look to the stars with humility and respect because your earth is about to have a reality check.

There is no death in earthly life, only transition, being reborn in the spirit.

Lessons of love, a reminder of our purpose here on earth; lessons to learn, so much more to life than we can see, to be concerned for our spirituality!'

Pass it on!

Electronic music continues to interest, with its exploration of yet more strange and wonderful sounds; but perhaps the biggest breakthrough is in an intensive and sustained exploration of the sounds of nature.

Highly developed, sensitised, sound recording equipment, strategically placed outside in deserted areas, wide open to the elements, has produced the most thrilling and unique sounds that equate to a huge symphony orchestra in full flight!

The pounding of wind and rain suddenly reduced to the soft, pitter-patter of raindrops; a deluge, a clap of thunder, yet more strong winds, gradually, slowly, turning into a gentle breeze stirring leaves and tall grasses into a rustle, a whisper, a pause – then, silence; the music of nature; poetical, magical, (and excellent for relaxation and meditation).

Holiday firms are encouraging business by following the trend, giving customers 'better deals' on whole family holidays, advertising; 'travelling with children, parents and grandparents, the extended family – and free baby-sitting!'

Have you noticed the Green Environmental issues appearing in television programmes; points made, such as in a situation comedy, drinking water out of a filter tap or bottled water, the actor carefully putting the empty bottle into a recycling bin. (Have you noticed how many people travel carrying a bottle of water these days, unheard of, not so long ago?)

• • •

Steve Robinson, from Merseyside, who works for United Utilities, generally uses radio waves to locate leaks – but sometimes tries two welding rods. A friend taught him water divining and now colleagues go to him for help.

Steve's comment: 'I've no idea how the process works, but it certainly gets results.'

• • •

In April 1968, on Broadway, New York, and later in the same year (and with the same creative team), in the West End of London, a new musical with the title *Hair* was produced. *Hair* opened to rapturous critical acclaim, a definitely 'stunned' public, and bearing a message that was 'confrontational' for the time, to say the least.

It was the first ever production with a mixed race cast, a 'huge' cast, and a cast who not only believed wholeheartedly in what they were doing, they 'lived it'. As critics observed in the original production, the cast were not 'acting', they lived their parts.

'You cannot be just an actor in this show. You have to engage your heart, mind and soul and do it every night.' These words are from the present director, Diane Paulus.

The musical, *Hair*, evolved from the 'hippie' movement in America in the sixties; the youth of America, especially those on college campuses, who started protesting against all that they saw as wrong with their country; racism, environmental destruction, poverty, sexism, violence at home and war in

Vietnam. Their protests, violent as they were, heralded in a new way of thinking and living which, forty years on, many now consider seriously, and some accept as the norm. *Hair* advertised as a celebration of life, love and freedom, and a passionate cry for Hope and Change.

'No discrimination, a global community, a return to simpler times, to natural things, natural remedies, no more selfishness', Love and Harmony, the message.

Pass it on!

• • •

January 2011. Tragic, and saddening to contemplate, is the terrible *shooting* recently in America of congresswoman Gabrielle Giffords and nineteen bystanders. With six of the bystanders killed, fourteen were injured, including the congresswoman, who miraculously survived suffering a bullet directly through her head. She is apparently making excellent progress.

Such is the reaction to this heinous crime, this attempted political assassination, that there is a call among people and politicians alike to 'clean up politics'; to make politicians more polite to each other, the media reporting that this tragedy could galvanise Americans to do politics in a different way. There is a call for a national debate about the use of harsh language and fierce rhetoric. The President, in his speech at a memorial service for the victims, called for people to meet each other with kindness, with kind words, not to be confrontational in our speech. 'To make sure that we are talking to each other in a way that heals, not in a way that wounds.'

• • •

The hippies wore colourful clothes from other cultures (a sign of the global community they envisaged); long, usually loose flowing hair, thought of as 'shocking' for men to sport, but again devised as a sign, a symbol, of 'expanding consciousness; a wanting to change things in order to create a more caring, back to basics society.

With regard to the musical *Hair*, the 'shocking' for the general public at that time, 1968, was the over-emphasis – for publicity purposes – on the nude scene, which, after all, was played out on a dimly lit stage and only lasted thirty seconds; songs celebrating hashish, LSD, free love, war-resistors, astrology, psychedelic drugs, 'rock'n 'roll'… . Thinking back to it, we see how far we ourselves have moved on from those – after all, 'not so far away' days – days of the late sixties, early seventies, as we consider and maybe better understand the challenge the show threw out to a startled public.

Amongst all the hype, and the decadence, however, the 'boisterous' publicity, and tales of 'rough' living, can we now see more clearly the true spirit of the New Aquarian Age trying to emerge? 'Bursting' to make its presence felt in the world, and what more public place to appear than in the theatre, engrossing people in the action, singing along, tapping their feet to the catchy tunes, some of which made the 'Top Ten' list both here and in America, and indeed all over the planet.

• • •

Christmas morning 2010 and Tommy, ten years old, had a new computer game amongst his presents, 'Sports – Konnect'. The idea being to first insert your own name, and then the computer brings up the name of your opponent, and 'off you go'.

The young lad, on inserting his name 'Tommy', let out a cry of bewilderment and surprise as the name of his opponent appeared.

It was the name Lena. Lena, the name of an aunt, his Aunty Lena, who had died two years previously.

Tommy got an extra, very special present on that particular Christmas morning, one that he will perhaps only fully appreciate later on in life.

• • •

The return of *Hair* to the West End stage in 2010 after forty years, and the excitement it has generated, is still as palpable as it was all those years ago. Not because of the 'shock and horror' it created for those first audiences; and not because we can, years on, turn a blind eye to those explicit scenes (explicit for the time), see them for what they are, but because of the 'message'. The message that finally 'took root', and is – however 'shaky', becoming evidenced every day around the world.

> *Harmony and Understanding,*
> *Sympathy and Trust abounding,*
> *No more falsehoods or derisions*
> *Golden living dreams of visions,*
> *Mystic crystal revelation,*
> *And the mind's true liberation.*
> *Aquarius.*

One of the writers of the show, James Rado, explains how he was very drawn to the idealism of the hippies.

'I felt it was almost a spiritual cause.' People were communicating in their own way, they were letting their hair grow, trying to form a new culture, a new way of living based on this notion of love, for humanity, and for each other in person.

Hair was conceived almost in a 'missionary' spirit.

• • •

For centuries, prophesies predicted the end of the world in the year 2000, but it seems to be that the many more (prophesies) predicting, far from being the end of the world, that the year 2000 would herald in a New Age for humanity, appear to be happening.

Is it because of the dire circumstances surrounding us that trends in society are changing fast – social, environmental, cultural, political, economic and religious? Perhaps the key word uniting all these changes is 'unity'. Unity – and another characteristic of this new age would appear to be the determination of people, all over the world, to have their 'say'. There is an urge for greater participation.

'When Amnesty International was born in 1961 it was greeted as "one of the larger lunacies of our time". How could ordinary people, by writing polite letters to governments and dictators save the lives of people they had never met? Today (this was written in 1990), with nearly three-quarters of a million members in over 150 countries it has adopted 30,000 cases of political internment. All these cases are the fruits of a greater consciousness of our human worth.'[4]

Human Rights campaigners (belonging to all sorts of organisations), and the 'will of the people' is sometimes called 'people power'.

January 2011 and we are witnessing so much unrest in the world; disease, tragedies, natural disasters (some of near Biblical proportions), as reported in news stories. With a struggle for social justice in one country, fighting on the streets for freedom in another – where even pacifist monks, outstanding in their saffron robes, gave support to the people, simply by their presence; the world is in turmoil. Fairer financial regulations, equal rights, climate campaigns, including environmental social justice, protest movements of one sort or another, words that we are becoming familiar with as they head the news in our fast-changing (world) society.

Sweeping along with all the major changes are many of the

small familiarities with which we are accustomed, touching on just about every aspect of our lives. Home, work, health, leisure, holidays; but this is the nature of change; the wearisome, laborious, shedding of what is – 'out of date', no longer viable, no longer necessary, in this 'new age' struggle to be born. (An age predicted, remember, to become one of unity, harmony, the brother hood of man, enlightenment!)

Pass it on!

• • •

Donna and Mark were driving along a dark, lonely road when she called out, 'What was that?'

'What was what?' Mark replied.

Donna: 'I just saw a naked woman lying in the road back there, go back.'

They returned but saw nothing. Mark walked over to a steep embankment, looked down, and saw a car lying on its side at the bottom of the hill.

The police were called, and when they arrived, it turned out that the car had been there for days. The woman driver was dead, but her young three- or four-year-old son was still alive next to his mother.

Donna believes that what she saw was the ghost of the mother seeking help for her son.

• • •

There is a new, worldwide show of 'unity within humanity' occurring; (we saw it in the eighties with the overwhelming response to 'Live Aid', and 'Sport Aid', when millions of people across the world expressed a great outpouring of love and concern for the millions of starving people in Africa), and all this through the medium of television.

Through the medium of television, 'perhaps for the first time on planet earth we witnessed the potential of the power of goodwill as a mass force'.[4a]

A new, worldwide show of 'unity within humanity', which, because of the access to information technology, is a networking facility that is hurrying in changes all over the globe.

President Nelson Mandela of South Africa recognised the value of the new technology back in 1994, when he spoke to the US Congress:

> 'As the images of life lived anywhere on the globe become available to all, so will the contrast between rich and poor within and across frontiers, and within and across continents, become a motivating force impelling the deprived to demand a better life.'

President Mandela continued, then ended, by saying, 'This may mean that technology will do what all the great thinkers failed to do – prove that "we are all part of one, indivisible and common humanity".'[5]

The social media; telephone-communications, texting, radio, internet, 'technology', all hurrying in the badly needed changes to the way of life all over the world.

Dr. Shershah Syed, a surgeon and gynaecologist, visiting a disaster area (whole devastation through the recent floods in Pakistan), believes that this latest crisis might lead to long-overdue social change, commenting that 'disasters might focus the world's attention to the plight of the poor'.

President Obama, after the recent dreadful shootings in America calling for people to be 'kinder' to each other, to be more careful in our choice of words; to use words that (help) heal, not wound.

Rioting in the streets in one country after another as even the most ardent of pacifists, and the shy, and the old, and the sick, join with their fellow countrymen in a show of unity, of strength, fighting for their political freedom, for social justice; in other words, for a better way of life.

It appears that humankind, having got away with too much for too long, is at last having to face the consequences of greed and selfishness; of paying homage to a 'fully-charged', materialistic way of life, ignoring the spiritual, at our own peril. (There is a thought that, although the world is more materialistic, humanity as a whole is becoming more spiritual!)

> 'We live in times of momentous change. We are spiritual beings, and our survival depends on connecting with ourselves, each other and the world around us.'[6]

To recognise our spiritual / human, worth; and perhaps natural catastrophes have brought to light the fact that we are not the masters of the world and all that is in it and above it and below it, but that we are 'partners'. We are partners with nature – not owners.

Pass it on!

The new 'Age of Enlightenment' is not only teaching us how to live in harmony with each other (The Brotherhood of Man), but is crying out to us the message, 'Right the wrongs done to the natural world'; live in harmony, not only with each other but with the whole of creation.

Pass it on!

> 'The growing awareness of this is manifested in the campaign against blood sports, the complaints about

factory farming and battery hens; the outcry against vivisection, the movement for animal welfare. Of the increasing number of people today, for different reasons, becoming vegetarians.'[7]

• • •

For some time I have experienced an extraordinary contact with what I may call some 'power' or guidance outside my ordinary day-to-day life.

To solve the many problems that we all have to face I find that 'organized' religion is useless, but in some quite unexplainable way my long search for 'light' seems to be leading me to what I most need. I can now contact the vast storehouse of power that comprises the universe.

By concentrated, voiceless prayer and, in a way, relaxation, I may feel my whole spirit filled with this power, and my whole being recharged.

When this happens, then I know that anxiety, troubles and so forth will be solved: and indeed they are.'[8]

• • •

A new, all-embracing shift to 'love and harmony', care for each other, for all life, recognising *all* life as belonging to one creative force, is gradually seeping its way into our lives. Of that, there is no doubting, and it is making a difference, proving, in at least one way, that we have now 'arrived' and are adhering to the new age.

As mentioned in an earlier chapter; as more emphasis is placed on teaching good citizenship in schools, and this including the very young, so children are being taught to respect *all* life, 'mini-beasts', bees, ants and worms.

Good news stories pushing their way to the fore, as in the story of Boz and Mickey, two Jack Russell terriers, who saved

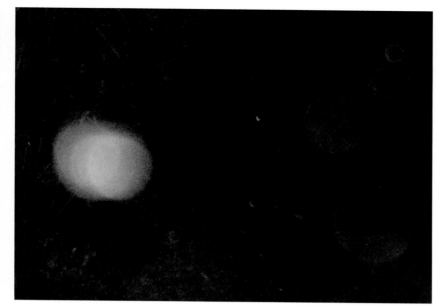

1) The camera, pointed into an almost dark, winter's night, in woods, produced this beautiful blue image.

2) Another night, and the same woodland area, and again with darkness approaching, Linda did not know what, if anything, she would capture as she focused her camera.

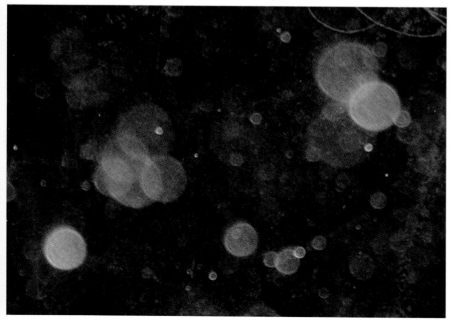

3) The stained glass window with orb is from the now completely restored twelfth century church of the Augustinian Priory at Brinkburn, Northumberland.

4) The large, search-light effect of the centre orb is particularly interesting. This photograph, taken in, yet again, near darkness, and in the same woods.

5) A host of orbs as back-drop for three grasses; this photograph again taken in near darkness, in the woods, somewhere in Northumberland.

their owner from certain death through hyperthermia, cuddling up to him for sixteen hours, refusing to leave him, after a bad fall left him slipping in and out of consciousness.

Sad but thought-provoking, the recent story from Africa of baby elephants trapped on a railway track, killed, along with other elephants trying to save them...a blackbird killed, lying on the edge of a pavement, with other blackbirds hovering and circling around frustrated, as if trying to help; or were they simply saying 'goodbye'.

As in all human life, there are tales of bravery, love, loyalty, or simply 'caring', coming from the animal kingdom. Tales which we hear about, read about, and perhaps 'think' about as never before...raising ourselves out of the mire of cruelty and destruction (which includes the whole of nature), and off the road to 'Nowhere' a place which we in the world have been cornering ourselves, for such a long time.

Young people are rising to the challenge, as they too become ever more aware of the part they must play in saving our planet from self-imposed destruction, appreciating the world we live in, and organising protest and conservation movements to save what is, after all, our natural inheritance. Travelling to far-away places, they quickly bond with the local society, work in poor areas, and by their 'goodwill' and compassion, follow the creed that our survival depends on 'connecting with ourselves, each other, and the world around us'.

Pass it on!

• • •

'My daughter Joan was killed by a car when she was seven years old. She and I were very close and I was grief-stricken. She was lying in her coffin in her bedroom. I fell on my knees by the bedside. Suddenly I felt as if something a bit behind me was so overcome with pity that it was consolidating itself. Then I felt a touch on my shoulder lasting only an instant, and I knew there was another world.'[9]

• • •

This new, collective, love and harmony, care for each other, 'spirituality'; the recognition of *all* life as belonging to one creative force which is seeping its way into more and more lives, and making a difference, is 'The New Age Movement'.

Bookshops and general stores are full of books on the subject; the green environment, health and alternate therapies; meditation, dreaming, Angels, Fate and Fortune – and people are reading them! It is particularly interesting to note that now, many of the well-known bookshops have separate shelves, in some cases different compartments, all well marked, to differentiate between 'religion' and 'spirituality'.

The new age thinking is more than a new age of social concern or of global politics, or fairer economics. It is a growing of consciousness, leading to a new way of understanding life and religion; realising that to be religious is not necessarily to be spiritual, or vice versa. (The realisation that we don't have to belong to any church or religion to be spiritual.)

Many authors see the new consciousness as being born out of a natural expression of 'intuitive thinking'. Intuition: power of knowing without reasoning or being taught. It is 'Inner Wisdom'.

With this new consciousness comes the understanding that we are spirit, here and now, in a physical body (which we need to inhabit the earth plane). We are beginning to appreciate our own true worth; we are beginning to 'feel' that we belong to something greater than any material, or physical force; that we link into 'something' beyond us, greater than we could ever imagine and yet, amazingly, of which we are a natural part.

We are now starting to 'take the reigns' in our own lives and in society. To 'think' for ourselves with a self-belief that is not afraid to admit to the power of 'thought' (thoughts are living things). We are not afraid to express our belief in 'prayer' and see a message in a coincidence and know the reality of dreams, and that there is a reason for everything and that the time for change is upon us and that...*the spiritual will no longer be ignored*...All this evidenced in so many ways as we 'see', begin to understand, and as we move deeper into the light.

Pass it on!

• • •

My husband Bill and I were out walking and we were talking of an especially close friend who had died when suddenly I knew that his spirit lived, and was as close to me that moment as it had ever been in my life. When I say 'I knew', words are inadequate to convey the experience. This was 'knowing', more vivid and real than anything I had ever experienced in the literal sense. It was as if for a moment one had known reality, and in comparison the world of the senses was a dream.

I was filled with an unutterable joy, which I shall never be able to describe.[10]

• • •

Under the heading, 'Germany's religious motorway 'services', Steve Rosenberg explains: 'In the middle ages, travellers and pilgrims had wayside chapels where they could stop and pray. Today, Germans have motorway churches; rest stops for body and soul.'[11]

Moving onto exit 39, on Autobahn 9 (Germany's motorway), the ringing peal of church bells generates a welcoming sound for weary travellers.

Saint Christopher's, one of more than thirty official motorway churches in Germany, are rest stops for body and soul. Here, at Saint Christopher's, as on any one of the other religious motorway stops, you will find an assortment of travellers from Doctor Juerg, who has stopped for a few minutes prayer – 'Life is too fast, I want to feel the quietness again' – to Arthur, the head of a textile company. 'I drive very much, and if there is time I stop to have a talk with God.'

Wolfgang Fritz, who runs a construction company, explains why he makes time to stop at exit 9. 'In my life I have to fight all day; in the construction business, we fight about everything. But I also have to fight to stay a human being.'

Some of the motorway churches are Catholic and some are Protestant but they are open to people of all faiths, all drivers, seeking a few minutes 'peace'.

Arriving at exit 76, the church there has a little water fountain and peaceful music playing to help people relax. Wolfgang Schuck is lighting a candle. 'It's a stressful job driving trucks. I'm on the road three or four days a week. You've got to find time to relax so I try to come to this church once a month to help me find inner peace; to escape the craziness of daily life.'

To relax, find quiet, searching for inner peace, these churches are welcoming people of all faiths and denominations, weary travellers on this earthly journey of ours.

Communities everywhere, are being welcomed, 'encouraged', into churches for any number of social activities as the premises (many are buildings of great traditional stature) are feeling the 'pinch', especially in these present difficult financial times. But is this situation not part of the grand design for the 'new age', bringing people together? – Doors that might have been open to six or seven now attracting dozens and more, and giving the opportunity to those perhaps previously 'shy' of entering, say, a large, grand church 'another' reason to do so; and who knows where that might lead.

A Methodist Church, one among hundreds of others up and down the country probably doing the same thing, has, in the last few years, opened its doors for a weekly 'luncheon club', under the leadership of a retired policewoman wanting to 'help', to give something back to society. It has been so successful that the church is able to give a substantial donation to charity each week from the proceeds, and for many of the customers, the luncheon club is the 'highlight' of their week.

(The same church, under the same leadership, organised a 'bonanza' of a Christmas day for 2010. Laying on transport where needed, the visitors arriving early for breakfast, followed later by morning coffee and biscuits, socialising, Christmas dinner with all the trimmings, entertainment, afternoon tea, all wrapped in the best of joviality and companionship, making it the happiest Christmas ever, for all concerned.)

Cardinal John Henry Newman, soon to be canonised as a present-day saint, was an outstanding scholar but whose care for people was fundamental to everything.

Cardinal Newman, born in 1801 and died in 1890, was one of the most distinguished English Catholics of the nineteenth century.

He was a man of deep faith, always searching for truth, and with a passion for education in what he called the 'large sense of the word', what we might call, culture. He was, however, through his care and concern for people, at heart a pastoral priest, and he was a parish priest for over thirty years.

As a young man, while abroad, and in a moment of depression, he wrote what is perhaps the most popular, and best known, of all hymns, 'Lead Kindly Light'.

Words carrying a strong message, appropriate for the world today.

Lead, Kindly Light,
amid the encircling gloom,
Lead Thou me on.
The night is dark, and I am far from home,
Lead Thou me on.

'Lead kindly light. Seeking the light. Living with the light'…

Ever-growing numbers of people, countless numbers of people, and from all over the world, whose 'inner qualities' of love, compassion, justice, belief in the spiritual side of life as the true reality, are stepping forward, witnessing, therefore strengthening their hold (our hold) on the power for 'good' in life; ('good' being what it means to be truly human). They are 'light workers'; but who, or what, is a light worker?

You are a light worker, if you send out a kind thought, do a kind deed, remember to have a word with someone you think might be lonely; visit someone who you know is alone, phone them, just to let them know that you, at least, are thinking about them.

You are a light worker if, out of compassion, you include a stranger in, say, a 'gathering', a getting together, when you know that person seems to be 'left out', perhaps not wanted, for whatever reason, remembering the words of the old country and western song, 'a stranger's just a friend we don't know!'

You are a light worker if you say a few words of encouragement, give hope, give help, to one you know needs that bit of extra support; send out healing thoughts (they work) to a person not in the best of health and tell another that you will pray for them when you hear they have problems.

You are a light worker when you 'feed the birds', send a kindly thought out to *all* nature, all creatures, all creation (stargazing and moon-struck with the sheer magic of it all) – our world needs a lot of love. 'I've been loving you way too long but you are not loving me back' – words by rapper Kirk Nugent.

You are a light worker wherever you are, wherever you go, and to whoever you meet up with when you warm a heart with a cheery smile, exude a sense of 'welcome' with a hug, show how pleased you are to have met.

You are a light worker, when you care.

Pass it on!

• • •

'Soon after my husband died – I cannot say how long – a few days or even hours, I saw him crossing a plank bridge which had been thrown over a stream.

'The stream was in the midst of glorious country and there were fresh green bushes and trees everywhere. The plank was of old gnarled wood, not very wide and had evidently been utilized solely in order to get across the water. It was as simple as that.

'His pace was slow but very sure. He never turned round, yet I felt that he was aware that I was following at a distance.

'I could not see anything beyond his figure.

'I had no doubt whatever that he would be lovingly received when he reached his destination.'[12]

• • •

A quietly strong revolution is taking place in our world today. It is happening now, as I write these words, and as you read them.

Across oceans and deserts and cities and towns and villages, tiny hamlets and solitary places, high mountain ranges and green prairies, cold regions and hot, everywhere, dramatic changes of near catastrophic proportion are taking place; dramatic changes that are heralding in the 'new age', the age of Aquarius.

The new age, in which it is said that humanity will be forced to move onto a higher consciousness, 'awareness', changing our way of living to a more spiritual, less materialistic, selfish society.

(Remember the story of the people of Atlantis who were so clever, so technologically advanced, with wealth beyond measure, living in a futuristic, high luxury society, and so completely absorbed with power and greed and selfishness that they forgot their 'true selves'. During the course of one day and night their home, the island of Atlantis, was 'swallowed up by sea' and vanished.)

We cannot avoid the changes that are happening in our world today, but we can be part of the crusade to see that the 'changes', and what happens in the aftermath of the changes, will be for the better.

Slowly but surely, we are being forced out of the dark shadow cast over our beautiful world by the self-destructive forces of greed and selfishness, to answer the call of our higher nature, our 'true self', our inner self. A new awakening of our spiritual nature being the saviour, 'not only of the planet', but also being the means of enriching our own personal happiness as we move to feeling a more 'connectedness with others', and with *all* life, in Love and in Service, and in Understanding.

(Madagascar is one of the poorest countries in the world – the natives are no longer hunting the exquisite little lemurs but trying to save them; they have been hunted almost to extinction, explaining why they did it in the most poignant words, 'We didn't understand.')

This is the last time for me to ask if you would like to make a note of anything you have read, or thought about, at the back of the book. The last time for me to ask if you have an experience you would like to set down, or maybe a dream, or a coincidence that turned out to be a message, a message, just for you. This is the last time for me, as you perhaps put a question into words, to ask you, to remind you, to be always 'open-minded', especially about things of 'the spirit'.

Spirit; as tangible as any material substance you will ever encounter; as 'real' as you yourself are prepared to accept it and your best friend in every moment of life; truly, your best friend.

In sheer 'joy', in pure abandon, child-like, let us hold our heads high, fling our arms open wide to the Universe, say a prayer, light a candle; send out *positive* thoughts raising our consciousness to the heavens.

Live in harmony, light, freedom and joy! Daydream, sit in the silence, meditate; love what is good.

Love nature; celebrate every crawling, hopping, buzzing, fluttering part of it.

Tell someone that you love them and tell them we are all 'loved beyond our understanding'...

Be happy...say a prayer...light a candle...

Be happy...light a candle...say a prayer...

Pass it on!

Is 'ORB' Photography Significant?

With the advent of the digital camera, orb photography has sprung up and blossomed into something of a 'people phenomenon', with almost everyone who has an interest in the 'game', whether professional or amateur, able to supply a picture with an orb on it.

It is exciting to relate that, after years studying the subject, many more scientists are taking the study of orb phenomena seriously, and a fair number are putting their 'weight' behind it e.g. 'It is great to know that we are receiving cosmic energetic communication': this from C Norman Shealy, MD, PhD.

Physicist William A Tiller, PhD adds his perspective to the unfolding adventure stating that he has 'come to the conclusion that the appearance of "orbs" in and around the planet earth at this time is not *accidental*'.

(Could this be in some way connected with the Age of Aquarius, the Age of Enlightenment?)

Tiller continues: 'My intuitive view is that it is a part of a heightening awareness brought about partially by the elevation in human thinking and partially by the increase in energies directed toward this planet by mostly benign life-forms existing in both traditional and untraditional (unseen) dimensions.'

He continues by saying that the orb phenomenon should be looked at as a positive experience for humanity, as just 'the first of a variety of communication manifestations to appear in the unfolding adventure of our future'.

Those words, found in the book *The Orb Project*, by Michael Ledwith, DD, LLD and Klaus Heinemann, PhD, a book packed with scientific – yet understandable to non-scientific minds – data, and scores of thrilling photographs and anecdotal evidence of 'orbs'.

Klaus Heinemann understands from his huge collection of evidence, that orbs delight to appear in happy family gatherings and that they try to communicate by the 'location' in which they appear in the photograph. He gives the example – this is in an interview with Hazel Courteney of the Times Newspapers Ltd – of a woman in the UK whose eighteen-year-old son died in 2007. Later, at her daughter's wedding, a bright orb appeared, by the bride's back. As with thousands of people who have seen orbs in their pictures after losing a loved one, Klaus Heinemann tells us, 'she believes this was her son letting her know that he was there for his sister's special day', and he also tells us his 'working theory' is that orbs are emanations from spirit beings...

'There has always been a huge body of anecdotal evidence that the spirit world exists, that consciousness survives physical death, and now, thanks to digital technology, we believe we are seeing it'.

'The Orb Project' claims to explore the 'spiritual realm' that can be seen in the stunning digital photographs published, and there is no doubt, in view of countless other world-wide scientific experiments taking place, that this is a phenomena now up for further, serious, scientific study (and debate).

We need to be cautious here, however; careful not to accept *all* orb photographs as emanating from the spirit side of life, to be sure we are not deluding ourselves. There can be other explanations for 'orbs', such as: reflections from dust particles or other minute debris in the atmosphere; milky-coloured ones can be reflections from water vapour particles; it could be flare, caused by grease (from finger marks) on the lens, made visible by the flash – if used, reflecting back from the window. In other words, according to other 'experts' in photography, there could be a number of 'conventional explanations' for the appearance of orbs.

As with any contact, or presumed contact, with the other side of life, we must be cautious and 'canny' in our findings – but always 'open-minded'. We need to weigh up the evidence carefully, even to our own 'mood', state of mind, at the time the photograph 'was taken'.

Four of the photographs in this book featuring orbs, are from woods in Northumberland, taken from dusk to almost dark, towards the end of winter 2010.

The 'photographs' were caught on a digital camera by Linda ——, who has kindly allowed me to publish them in this book.

Linda was amazed at what she saw when she printed the photographs, not knowing what to make of such a variety of beautiful colours and shapes and sizes and mostly taken after dusk. She took dozens of them.

But in trying to understand this phenomenon we now know as 'orbs', can we think back to earlier reading when we were trying to understand the meaning of being in a 'heightened state of awareness? – To the story of Rachael, a holiday representative in Mexico. Rachael was walking back to her hotel in the dark one night (not late), down a back lane, a short cut to a crossroads. Suddenly, out of the blue, in car head-lights that came up behind her, she saw a bald-headed man with a child on his back and other children around him. She described the little family in detail, and watched as they crossed the road in front of her, then disappeared.

Rachael's words about the experience are very profound – even though she insists knowing little, if anything, about such things. She said:

'It was as natural as if there are spirit people there all the time, around us, but suddenly an infra-red light comes on enabling us to see them, to "tune in".'

Not long before the experience, Rachael had suffered badly from a broken romance and was still trying to come to terms with it all. She was in a heightened state of awareness, therefore in a more sensitive state of mind, perhaps opening a door to another 'consciousness', 'awareness'; tapping into something very special we are rarely privileged to see.

Linda too was in a state of heightened awareness as she suddenly took off, alone, for the woods, in the cold almost dark night of winter. She too had much on her mind, going through a bleak, troubled time in her life and perhaps feeling that the silent, solitary, 'other worldliness' of nature, would provide some form of shelter and 'escape' for her troubled mind.

Her excuse for going out at that time of night, seems to have been to experiment with her digital camera; to see if anything of interest would appear in the approaching darkness.

Experts, on scrutinizing the photographs, all taken in woods in the same area, cannot seem to find any 'supernatural' significance in them except for one, maybe two, but all agree they are very 'interesting' pictures.

The third photograph, the one with the stained glass windows and 'orb', is from the now completely restored twelfth-century church of the Augustinian Priory at Brinkburn, Longframlington, Rothbury, Northumberland. The priory is set on a bend in the River Coquet, isolated, in beautiful scenery, in a heavily wooded valley.

Linda has taken dozens of photographs since that time, hoping to repeat some of the 'magic' found in those others, but has not been successful. Perhaps further proof that the significance of orb photography can often rest in our circumstances, *and,* on the determination of our loved ones on the other side of life, to make their presence felt in our hour of need.

References

*The Religious Experience Research Centre, University of Wales, Ceredigion, will be referred to as RERC in the following chapters.

CHAPTER ONE

1 Deepak Chopra, *Synchro Destiny*, p.18
2 Deepak Chopra, *Synchro Destiny*, p.125
3 'Highwayman', *Psychic News*, March 2009
4 Mary Bowmaker, *Is anybody there...*, p.47, Courtenbede
5 Bernard D'espagnat, *Psychic News*, April 2009
6 Ray Kennedy, from the so far unpublished, *Green Sand*.

CHAPTER TWO

1 The Society for Psychical Research, p.5
2 Colin Wilson, *The Giant Book of The Supernatural*, p.19
3 The Silver Cord, Ecclesiastes 12-6
4 'Phantom Arm', *Psychic News*, April 2009
5 Deepak Chopra, *Life After Death*, p.143
6 BBC, *Songs of Praise*, Summer 207
7 Penny Peirce, 'Frequency', *Cygnus* magazine
8 Sir George Trevelyan Selected Lectures: 'Awakening Consciousness'

9 John Micklethwait & Adrian Wooldridge, *God is Back*, Allen Lane

10 President Barack Obama, The Audacity of Hope, Canongate Books Ltd

11 Lyall Watson, *Beyond Supernature*, p.79, Bantam Books

12 Ralf Waldo Emmerson, *Creeds to Love & Live By*, p 7, Blue Mountain Press, Colorada

13 Lyall Watson, *Beyond Supernature*, p.209, Bantam Books

14 Lynne McTaggart, *The Field*, p295/6, Element

15 Lyall Watson, *Beyond Supernature*, p.75, Bantam Books

16 *The Sunday Times*, July 19th 2009

CHAPTER THREE

1 Lyall Watson, *Beyond Supernature*, Heraclitus, weeping philosopher, p.263

2 John Walsh Edgar, Cayce Centre Newsletter 51

3 Jess Stern, *The Sleeping Prophet*

4 Andrew Smith, *Moon Dust*, Bloomsburg

5 Lynne McTaggart, *The Field*, p.6

6 RERC, Seeing the Invisible, no 4764, p.171

7 RERC, no 1133, p.46

8 John Geiger, *The Third Man Factor*, Canongate

9 Lyall Watson, *Beyond Supernature*, p.168, Bantam Books

10 Alister Hardy, *The Spiritual Nature of Man*, p.151, RERC

11 Ann Petri, *Your Psychic World A – Z*, Arrow, 1984

12 *Psychic News*

13 Lyall Watson, *Beyond Supernature*, p.169/170

14 Andrew Smith, *Moon Dust*, p.197

CHAPTER FOUR

1 Ralph Waldo, *Trine In Tune with the Infinite*
2 Mary Bowmaker, *Is anybody there...*, Courtenbede
3 Antoine De Sainte-Exupery, *The Little Prince Egmont*
4 RERC, Seeing the Invisible, No 2062 p.73
5 Walter Nigg, Francis of Assisi, p.125 pub 1975, Commemorating the 750th anniversary of the death of St Francis
6 *ibid*
7 Mary Bowmaker, *A Little School on the Downs*
8 *ibid*
9 Lynne McTaggart, *The Field*, p.26

CHAPTER FIVE

1 Pamela Ball, *The Quantum Dream Dictionary*, p.24
2 S G Ousely, *Colour Meditations*, Fowler & Co Ltd
3 Marc Bekoff & Jessica Pierce, *The Moral Lives of Animals*, Chicago University Press
4 Andy Puddicombe, *The Sunday Times Style Magazine* – exclusive meditation
5 Alister Hardy, Society De Numine, Spring 2008
6 The Healing Buddha
7 RERC Seeing the Invisible p.143 no 3020
8 Franz Werfel, Austrian poet, dramatist, and novelist.

CHAPTER SIX

1 *Daily Express* 22/2/2010
2 Richard Lawrence, *Prayer Energy*
3 Eric Clapton, *The Autobiography*, p.237 & 257, Century, 2007
4 RERC. Seeing the Invisible, exp. No 4092

5 *The Scotsman*, June 2010, STV Today

6 Larry Dossey, MD, *Healing Words*, p.209, Harper Collins, 1993 (The power of prayer and the practice of medicine)

7 After seventy days trapped under nearly half a mile of rock, at midnight on Wednesday 13th October 2010, the thirty-three miners were safely, 'brought to the surface', one by one, in a tiny capsule specially designed to rescue them.

8 Psalm 46 V. 1.

9 Mary Bowmaker, *Is anybody there...*, p.106, Courtenbede

10 Tom Harrison, 'Thought for the week', *Psychic News*, Jan 2010

11 Former Air Chief Marshal Lord Dowding, *God's Magic*

12 Sir Alister Hardy, FRS, *The Spiritual Nature of Man*, RERC

CHAPTER SEVEN

1 James Rado & Gerome Ragni, words from song 'Aquarius', musical *Hair*

2 A T Mann, Millenium Prophecies, Element

3 Warren Buffett interview, *Fortune Magazine*, New York

4 Adrian B Smith, *God and the Aquarian Age*, p.27, McCrimmons Essex

4a *Ibid*, p.32

5 Charlene Smith, *Mandela*, p.6, Struik Pub (pty) Ltd, 1999

6 Revd Jonathan Robinson, *The Grail Liturgies*, Grail Barn, Churchstoke Pouys

7 Adrian B Smith, *God and the Aquarian Age*, p.35

8 Alister Hardy, The Spiritual Nature of Man, p.54, no 271, RERC

9 *Ibid*, p.42, no 165

10 *Ibid*, p.110 (no number)

11 Steve Rosenberg, 'Germany's Religious Motorway "services"', BBC News Berlin

12 RERC, Seeing the Invisible, p.93, no 4104